An Evening Among Headhunters

Our Like Will Not Be There Again

Hero Jesse

Smell of Earth and Clay

A Kayak Full of Ghosts

The Wrong Handed Man

Last Places

Wolverine Creates the World

An Evening Among Headhunters

& Other Reports from Roads Less Traveled

Lawrence Millman

Lumen Editions
a division of Brookline Books

ISBN 1-57129-055-9

Library of Congress Cataloging-In-Publication Data
Millman, Lawrence.
    An evening among headhunters : & other reports from roads less
traveled / Lawrence Millman.
      p.   cm.
    ISBN 1-57129-055-9 (pbk.)
      1. Millman, Lawrence--Journeys.   2. Voyages and travels.
I. Title.
G470.M517   1998
910.4--dc21   97-42463
                                                   CIP

Book design and typography by Erica L. Schultz.

Printed in USA
10 9 8 7 6 5 4 3 2 1

Published by
Lumen Editions
a division of Brookline Books
P.O. Box 1047
Cambridge, Massachusetts 02238
Order toll-free: 1-800-666-BOOK

CONTENTS

�֍

Islands Off the Map

In the Back of Beyond

PREFATORY NOTE

✿

During my travels in the Canadian Arctic, I once met an elderly Inuk (Eskimo) who told me this story:

Back in the 1930s, a missionary visited his camp and left behind a Bible. Not being able to read, he puzzled over this Bible for quite a while. At last he asked a friend to hit him over the head. The friend gave him a tentative tap that he barely felt. Harder, he insisted. The friend then gave him a clout that nearly knocked him senseless. After which, the old man informed me, "I understood the Bible very well."

The essays in this book make no such violent demands on the reader. Nor do they attempt to proselytize for an alien God, or even an alien god. If they proselytize for anything, it's for the farflung corners of the globe—long may they remain farflung, difficult of access, bug-ridden, assaulted by the elements, sweltering, hypothermic, and insular. Being somewhat insular myself, I'd rather spend my evenings in one of these corners, among (for example) erstwhile headhunters, than in bustling London, historical Rome, or Michelin-starred Paris.

These essays originally appeared, albeit in slightly different form, in the following publications: *Boston Review, Islands, Summit, Sunday Times* (London), *Che-Mun, National Geographic, Exquisite*

Corpse, Boston Globe, Providence Journal, Northern Raven, Passport,
and *North American Review.* Of the many editors I've worked with
over the years, I'd like to single out two, Joan Tapper at *Islands* and
Christine Walker at *Sunday Times,* for their passionate support of
my own passion for "roads less traveled."

I have not tried to update these essays to fit the convenience of
the present moment. If, for example, the island of Sark has undergone a bloody coup since I wrote about it in 1990, there will be no
mention of it here. For this, I beg the reader's indulgence and ask
that he consider my essay a window on Time as well as Place.

— Lawrence Millman
Cambridge, Massachusetts
August, 1997

LAWRENCE MILLMAN

Never be flippantly rude to elderly strangers in foreign hotels. They always turn out to be the King of Sweden.

—SAKI

You can only stay in your motel room for so long with your Gideon Bible—then you got to go outside.

—JONATHAN WINTERS

TROPICAL
LANDFALLS

BOOKLESS IN BIAK

Once, in the Ecuadorian Amazon, I was obliged to lighten my baggage prior to boarding a seemingly lighter-than-air plane. I wouldn't have minded giving up my waterproof poncho, my hiking boots, and my chloroquin tablets, but when the pilot asked me to leave behind Waterton's *Travels in South America* and Alec Waugh's *Hot Countries,* I became rather upset. What if I were laid up in some remote jungle hut? I wasn't worried about dying, but I was worried about dying without a book to read.

Of all the maladies capable of striking down a traveler in a foreign land—malaria, blackwater fever, typhoid, sleeping sickness, and so on—the one I fear the most is being caught with nothing to read. Let the monsoons play havoc with my itinerary, the national airline go on strike, and the foreign land itself prove unabashedly dull: a good book or indeed a bad book will always save the day. Nor do I even need to open this book. Simply the knowledge that it's there, waiting to be opened, is enough.

Not too long ago, on Biak Island off Irian Jaya, I turned the last page of Charles Darwin's *Voyage of the Beagle.* I wasn't too concerned about this because I figured I still had an unread copy of Graham Greene's collected short stories lodged somewhere in my rucksack. I was mistaken. There was no Graham Greene in any pocket, nook, or corner of my rucksack. There was no book at all, in fact.

I was still more or less unperturbed. Biak is not the North Pole or the nether Sahara but the gateway to eastern Indonesia, and thus an important traveler's way station. My bookless condition would only be temporary. Or so I told myself to keep up my morale.

My first thought was to visit the airport. Like other airports in Irian Jaya, it doubled as a concession stand and sold such native curios as spears, carvings, and charms made from chicken feet. I figured it'd sell books, too. I even imagined finding a copy of Peter Matthiessen's account of his 1961 Irian Jaya trip, *Under the Mountain Wall*, a book I'd always wanted to read. Or failing that, I'd buy a thriller or two, preferably by Simenon, whose Inspector Maigret novels I'd been able to pick up in such farflung locales as the Outer Hebrides and Coeur d'Alene, Idaho.

Sad to say, the concession area of the airport was closed. It opened only for international flights. The next such flight, I learned, was two days away and happened to be the flight I was booked for. Those two days suddenly loomed before me like ten years in a Siberian gulag.

I hopped a *bemo* for Biak Town, otherwise known as Kota Karang, City of Coral. Here, among an assortment of shacks and jerry-built houses, among Chinese traders, Indian tailors, and Javanese durian merchants, among ubiquitous piles of penis sheaths ("You wish to try on?" one waggish salesperson asked me), I looked for something akin to a bookstore.

An hour's search turned up no local equivalent of B. Dalton. It didn't even turn up the local equivalent of a drugstore or a newsstand. In fact, it didn't turn up any printed matter at all. Well, that's not exactly true—a travel agency did offer me a colorful brochure on the beaches of Bali, along with an out-of-date ferry schedule for Yapen Island ...

The telltale symptoms of my malady were beginning to assert themselves. Palpitations. Profuse sweating. A sort of *horror vacui* taking over my thought processes.

Then all at once I saw a ray of hope—a small house with several books in the window. Eagerly, a bit anxiously, I entered what turned out to be a shop run by local missionaries. Its selection of titles consisted entirely of religious texts for school-age children. In my desperation, I probably could have managed a religious text, even one for a school-age child, but not a religious text in Bahasa Indonesia, a language I neither spoke or read.

The clerk was a Yapen Islander named Isaiah, one of perhaps half a dozen Isaiahs I encountered during my stay in Irian Jaya. I told this particular Isaiah my predicament. I'd settle for any book in English, any book at all, I said.

Isaiah knitted his brow. In those knit lines I saw my last hope dashed to pieces. Then he brightened. He went to the rear of the shop and brought down a book from an upper shelf. "You are maybe interested in bondage, sir?" he inquired politely.

I had an image of leather-clad missionaries gleefully tying up new converts and then having their way with them. It wasn't the right image for the book Isaiah handed me, however. This book was a dusty old Penguin paperback of Somerset Maugham's *Of Human Bondage*.

I'd read Maugham's novel at age sixteen and even then found it a bit cloying, long on sentiment and short on genuine drama. There was no telling what my reaction to it would be now, twenty-five years later. But I didn't care. I plunked down my rupiah, thanked Isaiah profusely, and strode out of the shop, my prize clutched lovingly to my chest.

Never mind that I ended up being too busy in Biak looking for cockatoos in a forest reserve and watching a firewalking ceremony in Adoki village to read *Of Human Bondage* again. Or even to crack it open for a single momentary brush with Maugham's prose. What mattered was this: at last I had a book in reserve, a buttress against the whims and uncertainties of travel, indeed, of life itself.

SOUTH SEAS REVERIE

It was in the Kingdom of Tonga, halfway through a life of somewhat befuddled politics, that I became a monarchist. This happened as I was watching the country's four-hundred-pound king, Taufa'ahau Tupou IV, descendent of the ancient Polynesian sky-god Tangaloa and thus inheritor of the world's oldest scepter, gamely row his exercise boat in Nuku'alofa harbor. What better, more innocuous activity for a head of state, I thought, than a display of public aerobics. Alongside His Majesty, happily treading water, was more or less the entire Tongan army. What a splendid use for an army, I thought to myself. Better, far better than sending it off to occupy some foreign land.

I remained steadfast in my loyalty even after I learned His Majesty had given Imelda Marcos a Tongan passport. *Imelda Marcos!* It seemed like a typically Tongan joke. For whatever would that shoe-loving woman do in these ardently barefoot islands?

———◆———

From his gingerbread Victorian palace in downtown Nuku'alofa, King Taufa'ahau rules over such a diversity of islands that it would seem to require a monarch of his considerable girth to embrace them all. There are islands built of raised coral, islands low-lying and scruffy, islands blowing out volcanic smoke, and even one island, Fonuafo'ou, that is sometimes completely under water. There's another island, Niuafo'ou, which is known as Tin Can Island because incoming or outgoing mail must perforce be sealed in biscuit tins and then carried to and from supply ships by swimming mailmen. Yet another island, Tafahi, lies so close to the jogged International Date Line that its inhabitants are the first people in the world to greet the dawn of each new day. Almost certainly one of Tafahi's vanilla growers will be the first person in the world to greet the twenty-first century as well.

There are islands where the matchsticks of outrigger canoes strake the beaches, and islands with beaches so empty the only marks are one's own footprints. Islands which seem to be composed entirely of pigs. Islands of women hammering paper mulberry bark into the ceremonial fabric known as *tapa*. Islands which boast the stores of the great South Seas traders, Burns Philp and Morris Hedstrom, and islands where nothing so exotic as a fruit stand, much less a store, exists. On one island, I was taken around by a woman, Faka'ilokimoana, whose name means "Report from the Bottom of the Sea"—her grandfather drowned just before she was born. On another island, I met a man who thought computers were musical instruments. He wondered: Do you squeeze them like you squeeze accordions, or do you strum them like ukuleles?

Two forces hold together this largesse of islands. First, there's the King, an absolute monarch whose word is law or soon becomes law once it passes through a parliament of handpicked nobles. Then there's the idea of *faka tonga*—the Tongan way.

A person who wishes to observe faka tonga will move slowly, almost imperceptibly, and structure his life in the simplest and most eloquent manner possible. He'll give what little money he makes to his neighbors or, more likely, his local church. He'll wear a wraparound pandamus-leaf mat called a *ta'ovala* or a knee-length *tupenu* skirt. Also, he'll eat foods like *sipi* (fatty mutton flaps) in enormous quantities, thereby promoting a national physiognomy not unlike His Majesty's.

And since Tonga is the only Pacific country which has never known the improving hand of European rule (selected benefits: loss of culture, depopulation, disease), perhaps in faka tonga there is strength.

Or if not strength, at least some remarkable convictions. To illustrate:

One day in Vava'u I took a taxi ride from the town of Neiafu to 'Ano Beach. After a while, my driver began complaining of a headache.

"Would you like a Tylenol?" I asked him.

"Thank you, my friend," he replied, "but I don't take drugs." Then he went on to tell me that the difficulty lay not with his head, no, not precisely, but with his Uncle Pinati. Actually, it lay with Uncle Pinati's bones. A casuarina tree was growing near the man's grave, and its roots were making his bones miserable. All he needed to do was visit this grave and cut away the roots, and Uncle Pinati would feel just fine.

Bouncing and careening, jolting and jarring, the taxi negotiated an endless series of potholes, any one of which could have given a person a very respectable headache ... only not in Tonga. In Tonga, family-strong and flora-rich, headaches derive from nothing so boring, so wholly unserendipitous as mere potholes in a road.

——▸◆◂——

Serendipity. I admit that I bent the sense of that word a little when I used it to describe a *pas de deux* between roots and one's uncle's bones. A more conventional definition, according to my dictionary, is "the faculty of making fortunate and unexpected discoveries by accident."

I made one of these discoveries the day I was shown the place outside Nuku'alofa where Captain Cook landed in 1777. Not only did Captain Cook land at this place, but he also took a nap here, my guide informed me. She pointed to a rather morose-looking stump—all that remained of the original banyan tree under which the Yorkshire navigator took his presumed nap. Then she grinned, as if to say: That's it. Tonga's tourist attraction. Not all that photogenic, is it?

Now comes the fortunate and unexpected part. I expressed an interest in seeing mulberry bark whacked into tapa, so we moved on to the neighboring village of Lapaha. Not long after we arrived, I noticed a man sitting cross-legged on a pandamus mat directly inside his doorway. I halted immediately.

Tongans have the unique ability to sit cross-legged on their pandamus mats for hours, maybe even days at a time, so that's not the reason I stopped. It was because I detected something vaguely familiar in this man's features. Where, I asked myself, had I seen that dignified and moral countenance, that strong brow? In retrospect, I realized I'd seen these features in old lithographs of Captain Cook himself. As it turned out, the man was the Reverend Samson Cook, a lay preacher in the local Wesleyan Church and a lineal descendent of the same Captain Cook whose stump I'd just visited.

Had the high-principled Yorkshireman sowed his seed abroad in the manner of his fellow sailors?

Not at all. Samson Cook gave me an account of his celebrated pedigree. His grandfather, Albert Edward, a nautical jack-of-all-trades and a whaler, was the fifth grandson of Captain James Cook, born fifty or so years after the latter's death in Hawaii. In 1885, Albert Edward was sailing from England to New Zealand when his four-masted schooner struck a reef off Tonga's Ha'apai islands. He managed to swim ashore and shortly thereafter, in the time-honored custom of shipwrecked mariners, took a local wife. From this

LAWRENCE MILLMAN

union came a prodigality of sons, all of whom Albert Edward educated in the art and craft of catching whales. One of these sons, Ned Cook, was Samson's father. From Ned, Samson himself learned this same art and craft, pursuing humpback whales in an open boat right up until the international ban on whaling in the 1960s.

"When the King told us about the whaling ban," Samson said, "I was sad ... sad to think that never again would I hear a whale say, 'Oh Mr. Cook, you have shot my heart.'"

Now it was this whale-catching reverend's turn to ask me a question. Why, he asked, had I come to Tonga? Obviously, I wasn't a missionary or one of those aid-bringing *palangis* (foreigners) with the E.E.C.

I could have given him a riff on Kipling's "For to admire an' see this world so wide," but dusk was already falling and my guide was impatient to get back. I stammered an answer:

"To visit *you*."

Whereupon the Reverend Samson Cook smiled benignly, even serendipitously, as his illustrious forebear might have smiled after learning that some Tongans had crept aboard his ship and stolen a couple of his personal effects, including his chamber pot.

——>•<——

Tongans are a people full of surprise, now easygoing and dotty, now deeply traditional and taboo-ridden. They use empty beer bottles, goldfish bowls, and university banners to decorate their cemeteries. They'll stomp their feet repeatedly on the ground to stop earthquakes. They eschew the impropriety of bathing suits and simply jump into the sea fully clothed. Half in jest but also half seriously, they'll tell you Christ was a Tongan.

On the subject of taboos, peer into virtually any Tongan backyard and you'll see a coconut thatch shed, usually of quite flimsy construction. Chances are, it'll be occupied—not by pigs or chickens but by one or more teenage boys. That's because the brother–sister taboo (eating together, sleeping under the same roof, and so on) is so powerful that once a boy reaches puberty, out of the house and into the backyard he goes, lest anything indiscreet take place between him and his sister. Teenage boys, indeed, are the lowest class of humanity in Tonga; at meals they get fed next to last, just before the dogs.

And yet Tongans are an exceedingly generous, even indulgent people. Consider the time I asked to see a *makafeke* (octopus lure), but somehow got the word confused with *fakaleiti* (transvestite). Sure enough, my Tongan host showed up an hour or so later with a fakaleiti. "No, no," I protested, "I want to see one of those rat-shaped lures I've heard about, the ones for octopus fishing." As it happened, the fakaleiti knew all about makafekes. Once upon a time (he told me) an unusually nasty rat left a scatological gift on an octopus' head, so ever since then octopuses have hated rats and attempt to drown them whenever they can. Hence the rat-like appearance of these lures.

Then the fakaleiti himself went out and an hour or so later returned with a makafeke so rat-like any octopus would have loved to hate it.

———◆———

The Friendly Islands, Captain Cook called Tonga, and the name stuck even though these same friendly islanders had been planning to kill him and, in all probability, eat him. Not, I dare say, everybody's idea of friendly behavior. In their defense, Tongans say they acquired this sort of behavior from Fiji, that murder is not at all faka tonga and that they've always preferred pork and taro root, not to mention sipi, to the putative joys of Yorkshire navigator.

It was in the Ha'apai archipelago where this murderous deed—forestalled, apparently, by an indecision over whether to do it after

LAWRENCE MILLMAN

lunch or after dinner—would have taken place. It was also in Ha'apai where almost the entire crew of the English privateer *Port-au-Prince* was killed in 1806. One of the few survivors, William Mariner, told the tale of this massacre to a London physician named John Martin; the resulting book, *An Account of the Natives of the Tonga Islands,* remains the best ever written about the alternately murderous, alternately ingratiating habits of Tongans.

No attempts were made on my own life when I visited Ha'apai myself. Far from it. Everywhere I went in these palm-clad, beach-girt islands, I was greeted with twinkling eyes and a smile, armfuls of fruit or a mat in the shade, and always, *always,* whether I was coming or going, delighted shrieks of "Bye, bye, Louie." That line, from a radio commercial for Raid bug spray, was the only English most people seemed to know.

To call Ha'apai languid would be to imply a level of abandon far beyond its normal pace. There's a story about an Australian engineer, a man named Doolittle, who once fetched up on the capital island of Lifuka. "Your name, Doolittle," he was told. "It's so beautiful. You must be one of us."

Whole days pass here with the only noise being a pig rustling the brush or a rooster exercising its raucous larynx. At any given moment, half the population seems to be strumming ukuleles or catching a snooze under a palm tree. Fishermen tie hook and line to a coke bottle, bury the bottle in the sand, and then retreat to the nearest palm tree themselves. If you asked them about this, they'd cite the infinite superiority of *m'ui nonga,* a peaceful life, to the sweat and rigors of work.

One day I joined a Lifukan family for a picnic on the uninhabited island of 'Uoleva. At an American picnic, there'd be volleyball, frisbees, swimming, maybe some beachcombing. At this picnic, the girls juggled guavas (*hiko,* or juggling, is the favorite sport of Tongan females), but that was it. The men and boys slept. I got the distinct impression that both sexes thought life too precious to waste in meaningless flailings and wrenchings of their bodily parts. Like Zen Masters, they aspired only to a condition of repose. And the vast quantities of food we consumed—pork, fish, breadfruit, plantains, papayas, yams, cassava, coconuts—encouraged this repose, nay, insisted on it.

"Sit down, sit down," Ha'apai people always seem to be saying, as if even standing up were an arduous endeavor, and one evening I sat down on the porch of my beachfront *fale* to find my host's aunt and uncle sitting there, too. They'd heard I was feeling bad (I'd strained a ligament), so they were here to cheer me up. They sang me songs about His Majesty, the Crown Prince, local fishing, and the wondrous rotundity of local pigs. They sang sweetly, gently, in lilting rhythms, to the soughing of wind in the tops of palm trees. And I was so transported that I wouldn't have minded at all if they'd killed and eaten me after the last song.

In the 1830s His Majesty's great-great-great grandfather Taufa'ahau, High Chief of Ha'apai, later King George Tupou I, swam through a cut in the Ha'apai reefs and shouted defiance to all sharks. He waited. Nothing happened. The sharks neither ate the High Chief nor otherwise mutilated him. So much for the reputed powers of the Shark God. Henceforth Tonga would be as devoutly Christian as previously it'd been devoutly Shark. Henceforth, too, Sunday would become a day of such universal rest that it would make Sunday in a Presbyterian church seem like a riotous bacchanal.

One Sunday I took a boat from Lifuka to 'Uiha, the island just beyond 'Uoleva, with the local Catholic priest. As the priest was saying Mass, I walked around and regarded the lofty spiritual plane of a Tongan Sabbath. It is a day when flights do not fly; fishing is prohibited; digging taro root is prohibited; and acts of public agnosticism, like hanging up your wet laundry, are punishable by fines. Even Seventh Day Adventists, who elsewhere consider Saturday a day of rest, observe Sunday in Tonga and rest accordingly.

From one end of 'Uiha to the other I walked, passing the Catholic Church, the Wesleyan Church, the Free Wesleyan Church, the Mormon Temple, and the Church of Tonga. The last of these, especially, struck my fancy. It had turrets and battlements and slitted holes for archers. Later I found out that a 'Uiha man once visited Disneyland and was so impressed that he drew up the plans for the new church back home based on the somewhat irreligious model of Sleeping Beauty's Castle.

Never was I out of earshot of a hymn, a service, choir practice, or the thumping of a *lali* drum to announce one of the above. Nor did I see anyone else even remotely ambulatory except en route from home to church or going home again. Yet the varnish, I thought, was thin, easily chipped away. There seemed to be the same profound casualness, the same spirit of m'ui nonga, to all this sitting and singing, this communality, that I'd observed during the rest of the week. Except that now it was church-sanctioned—a blessing put around the urge to make one's voice melodious and to arrange one's body in the most comfortable of postures.

In the wooded northern part of the island, I was searching for the stony ruin of Makahokovalu (an ancient pigeon-catching site, I'd been told) when suddenly there came a loud snort. I readied myself for a stern-visaged 'Uihan to inveigh against my misconduct on the Sabbath. Then the snort materialized; it belonged to a large black pig who'd been busily rooting up the brush. We gazed at each other for a moment. Then the pig went his way and I went mine, two apostates in a land of sublime indolence.

North of Ha'apai lies the Vava'u archipelago, fifty or so raised coral islands clustered together so intimately that they appear to be a single island. Vava'u is justly celebrated by yachtspersons for its excellent harbors, unruffled seas, and coves so secluded they seem to invite an anchor. I wanted to find an *un*celebrated Vava'u-an island, so I asked a German who was a longtime resident of Neiafu, the archipelago's capital, one of my stock-in-trade questions:

"Assuming the law was on your trail, which island would you choose as a hideout?"

"Hunga," he answered without hesitation.

Off by itself, a high-cliffed solitary, Hunga is the least accessible island in the group. Whereas most of Vava'u's harbors are on the leeward side, Hunga's is tucked away inconveniently on the windward side. The Polynesian fisher-god Maui established it there, so the story goes, to discourage other Vava'uans from coming over and helping themselves to Hunga's immense bounty of pigs and produce. Thus does each island, however pocket-sized, believe itself a veritable Eden compared to its neighbors.

I hired a small boat in Neiafu to take me to Hunga. All went smoothly until we ventured beyond the Pule Pule Kai Passage; then the boat began to lunge and corkscrew at angles that defied the laws of gravity. I noticed that the boatman, a Hungan named Sione, hadn't bothered to pack any oars, life jackets, or emergency fuel. To pack such things, I knew, was not faka tonga. On the other hand, not to pack them struck me as *faka* risky, particularly with waves riding above our gunwales.

As politely as possible, I asked Sione, "What happens if we capsize?"

"We won't capsize," he said. "If there's trouble, we'll just float on over to Fiji."

"*Fiji??*"

"Yes. It'll take maybe two weeks. Have you ever been to Fiji before?"

Much to my relief, after some rearrangement of my semi-circular membranes and a bit of moistening from the sea, we made our eventual landfall on Hunga, not Fiji. Here, too, I encountered nothing but friendliness—gifts of fruit, an English-speaking schoolteacher to show me around, and swarms of kids eager to hold my hand. Soon I found myself eating a meal Tonga style: the guest eats first, then the women and girls, then the men, and then the teenage boys. This makes for a rather protracted dining experience, but no one ever accused Tongans of rushing a meal when they could linger over it for half a lifetime.

Yet I detected a slightly different atmosphere on Hunga than in Ha'apai. People would look me in the eye a little longer; women seemed to pound their tapa a little more insistently; the shrieks of "Bye, bye, Louie" were a little more aggressive; and kids reached for my hand with the assurance that they'd get it. When I mentioned this to the schoolteacher, she related the following story:

Many years ago so many people wanted to live on Hunga that something had to be done to keep their numbers down. Something *was* done. Baskets of food were flung over the cliffs at Fofua. Whoever could not retrieve one of these baskets was labelled a weakling and dismissed to some other part of Vava'u. Whoever managed to climb down and bring back a basket was allowed to settle here.

Present-day Hungans, the schoolteacher added, are descended from this fearless breed of cliff-scalers. Small wonder that their children grasp a visitor's hand with such assurance ...

Sione and I left Hunga at low tide. It wasn't long before I heard the unmistakable crunch of coral against the boat's hull. "It's too shallow for us to go through here," I said.

"Only if our hearts are shallow," replied Sione. He climbed out and began pushing the boat. He pushed it around one mine-field of coral after another until he got it safely to deeper water.

One should never question a Hungan boatman's heart.

⊰•◦•⊱

A few days later, I paid a late evening visit to a kava club outside Neiafu. There I joined one of several circles of Tongans seated on their pandamus mats. In each circle was a man pounding kava root between two stones, a man straining the pounded kava through a twist of hibiscus fiber, and a young woman ladling the finished product into a coconut cup. Each person was obliged to toss back this cup in a single swallow; two or more swallows would be considered an insult to the pounder, the strainer, the ladler, and the kava grower as well.

Derived from the *Piper methysticum* plant, kava tastes like a blend of liquefied mud and muddy rainwater, with a dollop of dental anaesthesia thrown in for good measure. Imbibing it, I felt as if I were running my tongue along the topsoil of someone's taro plantation and at the same time getting a cavity filled. But Tongans themselves aren't too concerned with the way kava caresses, or refuses to caress, their taste buds. They don't drink it to get drunk, either. Rather, they drink it for the quality of amiable serenity it imparts to their not necessarily unserene souls. One dedicated drinker told me that kava made him want to kiss all of creation, including *molekaus*. (A molekau is an eight-inch millipede capable of inflicting a very nasty bite.)

I confess that kava did not make me want to go out and kiss all of creation. There were still certain entities (Jesse Helms, *Amanita virosa* mushrooms, radio talk show hosts, and so on) which I deemed wholly unkissable. However, it did give me a curious sense of well-being, along with an equally curious sense of disembodiment. "You like kava?" the man sitting next to me asked. Palangis aren't supposed to like the drink at all.

"Tastes great. Just like the earth itself."

Cup after cup I drank, cup after cup the ladler ladled, until I felt myself far above the mundane world, treading space as if I were treading water. When at last I touched ground again, I was in a flyspeck country ruled by a monumental, aerobically-inclined monarch. It was a country where time seemed to be of no consequence, none whatsoever, and where ... but then my reverie of this doubtless fictitious place was interrupted. One of the kava circles was singing "Lead, Kindly Light" in such rousing fashion that it sounded like a fight song at a soccer match.

———➤◆◄———

Back in Nuku'alofa I decided to conclude my Tongan travels with a royal audience. The King himself had gone to New Zealand for his annual medical checkup, so I settled for an audience with the Crown Prince. Crown Prince Tupouto'a, current Minister of Defense and heir to his father's throne, was a more or less ordinary-sized person who spoke with a clipped English accent, a testimony to his Oxford education. Over a pot of jasmine tea, we chatted about a variety of topics: London's pubs and clubs; wolf hunting in Siberia; the mysterious attraction of raw jellyfish to the Tongan palate; and His Royal Highness' new villa, which he detested—he said it looked like a Howard Johnson's.

At one point we began talking about Tafahi. Aha, I thought to myself, here's an opportunity to score a hit on a sacred cow. So I said that Tafahi wasn't in fact the first place in the world to greet the new day. The first inhabited place, yes, but not the first piece of land. That honor fell to Big Diomede Island in the Bering Strait, which lies a hairsbreadth closer to the International Date Line than Tafahi.

"Well," the Crown Prince said, "we'll have to change that."

"How, Your Royal Highness?"

"By picking up Tafahi and moving it a couple of degrees closer to the Date Line, of course," he smiled.

I smiled, too.

For both of us knew that nothing in Tonga would change, much less be picked up and moved, for quite a while.

A DETACHED PART
OF THE WORLD

✽

With the decor of Paradise, as with cuisine, there is no disputing matters of taste. One person's caviar is another person's soggy dumpling. For myself, I've always preferred a good hearty slog over rugged terrain to the more easeful charms of the beach. Likewise, I've never thought the coconut palm—emblem of the paradisiacal tropics—any more interesting, of its kind, than the maidenhair tree, which smells like slightly soiled feet, or the arctic rowan, which after a hundred years is still only eight inches high.

So it was that upon my arrival in Rarotonga, capital island of the Cook Islands, I went for a backcountry trek rather than a stroll along one of the island's empty, palm-clad beaches. My guide for this trek was a man named Pa Teuraa. Dressed in *pareu* loincloth, barefoot, and wielding a machete, he looked the very model of an old-style Polynesian. Except for his dreadlocks. He wore his hair this way, he told me, so it'd be easier to wash. Then he pointed to a cluster of red flowerets which herbally-inclined islanders like himself use as a shampoo. He also pointed to the bright red flower, known in Maori as *ta'akura,* which definitely should not be used as a shampoo. It harbored the spirit of a woman by the same name who long ago was raped by some bloody-minded Rarotongan warriors. She died and, legend has it, passed into this flower. If you put a ta'akura into your hair, Ta'akura herself will appear and lure you to a death no less brutal than her own, usually, Pa said, by flinging you off a mountain or impaling you on a reef. Needless to say, I didn't put one of these pretty little flowers in my hair.

Rarotonga is a high volcanic island, with razorback ridges and dense jungle, more or less on the Tahiti design. And, like Tahiti, a few parts of its interior still have not been walked on by man or woman. Pa and I were not headed into these parts, but where we were headed felt almost as unfrequented. We traversed fields of thick bracken, crossed brisk streams, climbed muddy embankments, passed through disused taro plantations and the stony remnants of old villages, until at last we came to our destination—a boulder of undeniable heft and, according to Pa, undeniable religious significance. Here the Ancient Ones had worshipped their gods in premissionary times, probably as long ago as the great Maori voyages to New Zealand. Here, too, the Modern Ones seemed to have left some of their own gods, including empty rum bottles, worn-out sneakers, and a T-shirt which advertised *The Pacific Resort, Muri Beach, Rarotonga.*

I shook my head and got ready to be appalled. To think, rubbish in such a sacred place! But Pa said it wasn't rubbish, but offerings made by his fellow Rarotongans to propitiate the gods inside the boulder. See, even a couple of *arikis* (chiefs) had inscribed their names on the boulder's face.

"We call that graffiti," I told him.

"We call it giving a piece of yourself."

He too left a piece of himself or some sort of offering when he came here, and said I should do the same thing. So I left my socks, since they were covered with impossible-to-remove *kiri-kiri* petals anyway. And all at once, miraculously, socklessly, I felt much better. As if the gods were letting me know that they were indeed propitiated.

LAWRENCE MILLMAN

A curious group of islands, but just how curious? People honor the Sabbath even more virtuously than Scottish Highlanders, but they also honor Tangaroa, ancient god of fertility, whose well-endowed figure appears on their one-dollar coin. Their House of Parliament is no bigger than a convenience store and their government patrol boat is named, happily, *Te Kukupa* (*The Dove*). They change their own names whenever they like, to indicate the death of a sibling, a finger nipped off by a coconut crab, or perhaps just ownership of a motor scooter with a faulty clutch. They have a positive horror of rubbish, even a lone candy bar wrapper in the front yard, and yet they also inter deceased family members in this same front yard, a place they consider more intimate than a distant cemetery plot, not to mention more decorous than beneath the kitchen table (the former practice). And they call Japanese cars "Spam cars" because of their resemblance to the tins of a certain meat product—a meat product they consider a culinary delicacy second only to dog.

The Cook archipelago is strewn in leisurely fashion throughout the southern half of Polynesia; strewn as if by a Creator more attuned to the sounds of a coconut shell ukulele, all sweetness and lassitude, than to the demands of His own work ethic. From the air the Cooks seem to go on forever, volcanic islands, flat islands, atolls, coral *motus,* isles of copra and isles of pearl shell, no two alike. It took western navigators some 240 years to track them all down and even today there persists a rumor of one more as yet undiscovered Cook, a blessedly heathen atoll somewhere in the emptiness of the Pacific. Blessedly, too, the old beachcomber who told me about this atoll refused to tell me where it was, so that we could continue to nurture our fantasies of lost worlds, both of us.

"The most detached parts of the earth," Captain Cook called these islands, though he named them the Herveys, after the First

Lord of the Admiralty, rather than after himself. And detached they remain two hundred years later, not only from New Zealand, which governs their external affairs (they look after their own internal affairs), but also from each other. The northernmost Cook, Penrhyn, lies almost 1000 miles north of the southernmost one, Mangaia. Mangaia itself is Rarotonga's closest neighbor, but at 150 miles it's not what you'd call real neighborly.

Such distances make the fourteen inhabited islands of the Cooks feel like a crazy-quilt of small nations, each with its own traits and prejudices, instead of a generic country. We all know that Frenchmen are supposed to be excitable, Swiss industrious, and Swedes dour. Well, Pukapukans are supposed to be sexually exuberant and Mangaians sexually backward. Aitutakians are voluble, even glib, and love to argue themselves into untenable positions so they can argue themselves out again. Rarotongans are haughty, because it was from Ngatangiia Harbor, on *their* island, that the first great exodus of Maori canoes to New Zealand set forth. Maukeans, on the other hand, are docile and even a little stupefied, as befits a people with the unenviable reputation of being the only South Seas islanders ever known to dive for taro roots.

And what of the inhabitants of lonely Palmerston (pop. 66)? Ever since 1862, they've had a reputation for being Marsterses. Before that date, the atoll supported crabs, frigate birds, and bêches de mer, but no people. Then came an Englishman named William Marsters with his two Polynesian wives. He acquired a third Polynesian wife from a Portuguese seaman, whereupon he resolved to populate the atoll through his own initiative. The old fellow succeeded quite admirably in his endeavor. The present-day inhabitants of Palmerston, including the Reverend Bill, are almost all Marsterses, and the atoll remains the very best place in the world to go if you want to hear the speech of nineteenth-century Lancashire, England.

LAWRENCE MILLMAN

Concerning Atiuans, they were supposed to be unimaginably fierce, at least before the Apostle of the Pacific, the Reverend John Williams, calmed them down with Christianity. They would just as soon kill and eat a stranger as look on him. One of their favorite pastimes was to raid docile Mauke and force Maukean wives to eat their own husbands, though the selfish Atiuans kept the best cuts of husband for themselves. Even now the most common expression in the Cooks for a fight, ruckus, or just a quarrel is: *"E Atiu oki."* (It's Atiu trouble.)

But on Atiu I didn't encounter any trouble at all. No one gazed on me either with homicidal or gastronomic intent. Quite the contrary. I could hardly go anywhere without being offered a lift on someone's motor scooter; even huge boisterous mamas draped unsparingly over their vehicles would come to a rattling halt and invite me on. Nor could I go anywhere without a rich variety of foodstuffs being forced into my arms. The day I walked Atiu's version of the Appian Way, a coastal track overhung with ironwood trees and purple sprays of bougainvillea, I returned to my digs laden with breadfruit, taro, yams, and *utos* (coconuts germinated in the shell)—gifts from locals who figured that I must be a singularly deprived sort of traveler to be venturing out with just a camera.

Only Atiu's *makatea* keeps up the island's reputation for fierceness. One day I walked this makatea with a guide named Tangi Jimmy. Actually Tangi Jimmy walked, but I inched along delicately. Makatea consists of coral thrust up onto land eons ago and gradually fossilized, now into pinnacles and battlements, now into gargoyles no less fantastic than Notre Dame's. Parts of it are so sharp that if you fall down, you'll be carrying a souvenir of Atiu on your person for a long, long time. Other parts of it contain small grotto-like forests and even limestone caves. Tangi Jimmy and I were making our way toward one of these caves, Atiu's largest, called Anatakitaki.

It may seem odd that in the sunny South Pacific, I should be opting for the dark underground. In my defense I can only say that the sun is universal, the same blatant star whether it's shining in the Cook Islands or Cook County, Illinois. Anatakitaki, however, is the only place in all the universe where I'd ever see a *kopeka,* a species of swift nearly as rare as the whooping crane. No more than two hundred kopekas live in this deep, multi-chambered cave, navigating their passage through it with echo sounders, like bats. Once outside, they turn off these echo sounders and navigate more conventionally, though (tireless birds!) they don't land until they're back home in the gloom again.

Flashlights in hand, we entered this gloom ourselves and almost immediately began scrambling over boulders. Long palm roots, like strings, hung in our eyes. Stalactites also hung in our eyes. Because of these stalactites and the slippery-damp boulders, we had to move with a certain caution, looking up and down simultaneously, in a posture cavers call "the Groucho walk." After half an hour or so of this posture, we began seeing kopekas—small brown blurs hovering along the cave's calloused ceiling. They were sounding their echo devices repeatedly. *Click click click click click.* Soon we came to a large chamber so full of clicking that it sounded as if an orchestra of castanet players had taken up residence there. Now we switched off our flashlights and sat listening to this rather unusual concert. Tangi Jimmy told me about the time he'd gotten this far in the cave when all of a sudden his light gave out. On his hands and knees he had crawled back to the entrance by following the clicks of kopekas who were leaving the chamber themselves and heading outside for an insect dinner.

My last evening on Atiu I visited another local rarity, albeit a rarity less avian than cultural—a *tumunu.* A former cherished in-

LAWRENCE MILLMAN

stitution throughout the Cooks, nowadays tumunus survive only in the Atiuan bush. The word refers to the pandamus-thatch huts where men gather to discuss, for example, whether or not to put a new road through the taro swamp. It also refers to the home brew which fuels these discussions. Finally, it refers to the hollowed-out palm tree stumps in which this home brew, made usually from oranges, is left to ferment. Tumunus are supposedly illegal, but on the evening of my visit the island constable put in an appearance and threw back a few coconut cups of spirits himself.

The coconut cup went back and forth, back and forth, between the *tangatu kapu* (barman) and his increasingly less sober patrons. At one point the tangatu kapu asked all of us to bow our heads, and then he thanked the Almighty for giving us this home brew even as he asked His forgiveness because we were drinking it. At another point all eyes focused on me and I was obliged to give a speech, as is the custom with visitors, in praise of Atiu. Hardly had I finished this speech when a couple of lads with ukuleles and guitars broke into a lilting love song about their island. A love song about a place of dead coral, dank caves, and fermented orange juice! Somehow it did not seem inappropriate to my ears.

<hr/>

If Atiu rests at one pole, Aitutaki rests at quite another. Of all the southern, more accessible Cooks, it comes closest to the Hollywood image of a South Seas island. It has all the right amenities: a reef enclosing a turquoise lagoon; uninhabited coral *motus;* and any number of those proverbially empty beaches. It even gets swept over by the occasional hurricane, a sine qua non for a South Seas island in its Hollywood incarnation.

So it was that I flew to Aitutaki a bit fearful that I might be flying to Hollywood. But the island allayed my fears from the moment the Twin Otter landed—no, even before that moment, when it couldn't land due to the presence of crab hunters scampering around the runway. Also, it rained off and on, mostly on, during my entire stay, and there's no sweeter, more genuine sound in all the tropics than the patter of rain on corrugated iron roofs.

I arrived late on a Saturday. Next day I decided to explore the island, but that next day was Sunday and even Aitutaki's ubiquitous mynah birds seem inclined toward indolence on a Sunday. Thus I ended up exploring the island on my own, on foot, in a gauze of warm rain.

First I wandered down to the pocket-sized capital, Arutanga. Main attractions: a harbor that allegedly was Captain Bligh's last landfall before the *Bounty* mutiny, and a cheerful, slightly tumbledown lethargy few other capitals can boast.

Next I walked inland to the Marae Te Mangoa, a basaltic stone circle honoring, of all creatures, the shark: for it always was sharks, not frolicsome dolphins, who guided the old Polynesians from island to island or through difficult passages in a reef. After paying my respects to Are Mangoa, god of the sharks, I turned north and skirted one banana plantation after another.

Finally, I came to Maungapu, highest point on Aitutaki. At 407 feet Maungapu is no Everest, but it offered me a view which, I submit, could not have been improved upon by Everest itself. I was standing on the summit when all at once the cloud cover lifted and I saw all of Aitutaki's motus, a necklace of brilliant emeralds strung along a lacework reef. In the lagoon I also saw a solitary outrigger canoe occupied, my binoculars told me, by a seven- or eight-year-old girl masterfully flinging a fishnet into the water.

Later I visited Tunui Tereu, an Aitutaki storyteller, who told me this tale about Maungapu:

Once upon a time Aitutaki was only a dull, low-lying place. Locals figured they needed a mountain, so they swam the 161 miles to Rarotonga and hacked off the top of Raemura (the entire mountain was too big for them to hack off). This act of vandalism the

Rarotongans applauded, since now they had more sun and consequently more time to fish. The Aitutakians themselves held up the mountain with one hand, swam with their free hands, and finally made it back to their own island. They installed the top of Raemura just opposite Paradise Cove, where it has remained intact to this very day.

Tunui's wife seemed dubious. "I don't think even Aitutakians could steal a mountain," she said.

I was a bit dubious myself. But I changed my mind after I went to the Rapae Hotel's "Island Night." This included a floor show of lusty, hip-waggling traditional dances, but it also included a local man performing one of these same dances while husking a coconut ... with his bare teeth. Not since I'd seen the minister on the Scottish isle of Eriskay play the bagpipes and water-ski at the same time had I witnessed a more remarkable display of human talents. Stealing a mountain would be, by comparison, a piece of cake.

<hr />

The Cook Islands aren't what they used to be, say the *papa'as* (Westerners) who knew them in an earlier era. "Changed, changed utterly, old boy," the venerable Englishman said to me as we sat in Rarotonga's Banana Court Bar, a vintage Polynesian watering hole. But he seemed to accept these changes gracefully, all but one (to him) catastrophic change—namely, the demise of the old copra traders.

Thirty years ago you traveled from island to island in one of these delightfully squalid vessels or you didn't travel at all. And if you were fortunate, your captain would turn out to be none other than the legendary Andy Thompson, a rowdy, cantankerous, but wholly endearing character who once remarked that he could navigate anywhere in the Cooks simply by looking at the empty beer bottles he'd tossed to the ocean floor.

Maybe the Cooks *aren't* what they used to be in the old days. Or maybe, like Oscar Wilde's Oxford, they never were what they used to be. To chug towards a timeless Pacific isle in a rickety copra boat, with Captain Andy, perhaps drunk, perhaps not, at the helm—yes, indeed, that would have been quite an experience.

But I have a confession to make: for my taste, there are few approaches anywhere on this planet more exhilarating than when your plane sweeps down out of the clouds and, suddenly, miraculously, you see the lush green mountains of Rarotonga rising out of the sea like a landscape from a childhood fairy tale.

OF MAGIC STONES
AND WATER

✳

Pohnpei is not to be confused with Pompeii, the Roman city buried by Vesuvius, although there were times when I expected this island—the largest, highest, most dramatically florid in Micronesia's Federated States—to be buried by rainfall positively Vesuvian in its intensity. Down it would pour, down from the eruptive heavens, with the sound of a million wings beating the heavy earth.

At such times the island would feel nearly as liquid as the Pacific itself. Even so, it would never quite feel *of* the Pacific. For its 130 square miles have the heft of a small continent or a chunk of displaced Amazonia, albeit an Amazonia surrounded by acres of mangrove swamp. And imagine a Pacific island sufficiently large to possess an uninhabited interior—uninhabited, that is, except for a strange gnomelike creature called a *sokele*.

As I traveled around Pohnpei, I couldn't help thinking of Conan Doyle's Lost World. For the island, perpetually irrigated, seemed to burst forth with oversized anomalies: yams attained heroic proportions (I saw one specimen ten feet long weighing down the back of a pickup truck); grasshoppers looked large enough to mate with chickens; and huge ferns unfurled like opulent fans before my very eyes.

Or if not oversize anomalies, overrun ones: One day I found myself admiring what I took to be a gigantic tropical planter, only to realize that it was actually a discarded, terminally rotting Honda Civic. Vines cloaked its headlight sockets, and a guava tree was sprouting from its floorboards. On this occasion I also realized why Pohnpei, formerly a U.S. Trust Territory, used to be called a "rust territory."

But the longer I stayed on the island, the more inclined I was to dispense with the Lost World analogy. It seemed too facile for a place that was neither imaginary nor lost.

So, in the end I confused Pohnpei only with itself, an island wholly exceptional, with wholly exceptional scenes and images. Here a group of schoolchildren walked in the rain, each enclosed in a giant pandamus leaf. Here a wrinkled, bare-breasted crone suddenly donned a Fighting Irish T-shirt to conceal her nakedness. Here was an entire softball team adorned with magic amulets to avoid the curses of the opposition. And here rose the ancient city of Nan Madol, the so-called Venice of the Pacific, whose blocks of prismatic basalt reputedly had flown through the air, light as feathers, from their quarrying sites.

At first, I admit, nothing seemed to make sense. A guide showed up at my hotel two hours late, then apologized for being early. On a trek to a waterfall, my compass went haywire and kept pointing due south when it should have been pointing due north. In this most watery of places, the capital, Kolonia, had a water shortage. And what was that another of my guides asked me? It sounded rather like: "How do you cook your dogs in America?"

Then I showed up for an appointment two hours late myself. I hadn't been aware of my tardiness because the humidity left a constant cloud cover on my watch glass. So I took a lesson from this

LAWRENCE MILLMAN

and liberated myself from trifling matters, such as what time it was or even what day it was. I also liberated myself from the belief— quite erroneous on Pohnpei—that two and two equals four. I became lost in a love of my own aimlessness, or the island's, I'm not sure which, and began arriving at waterfalls, archaeological sites, and feasts without knowing exactly why or indeed how. Perhaps, like Nan Madol's stones, I flew.

Or if not flew, at least floated.

Consider the time I went for a trek near Nanalaud, Pohnpei's tallest mountain, in the island's uninhabited interior. "Another 'up,'" my guide would announce. And I'd climb a slope which required handholds on moss-covered tree branches and footholds on the same tree's slippery roots. "Another 'down,'" he would say. And then I'd slip and slide down a similar slope, usually garroting myself with vines in the process. Between these ups and downs, I'd slosh through ooze deep and primordial, seemingly bequeathed from the days of the earth's infancy.

At last I reached a bare rocky ledge no more than a foot wide. To my right was a vertical drop of at least two hundred feet.

"Traditional Pohnpeian test of manhood," my guide said.

Manhood, I knew, was not a matter Pohnpeians took lightly. It had to be earned. One test, called *lekelek,* consisted of the ritual lopping off of a 16- or 17-year-old male's left testicle by a *sou-n leik* (master cutter). If the victim shirked the knife, well, it was back to boyhood; but if he submitted to it, he had the Micronesian equivalent of chutzpah and from then on could have his pick of women.

Lekelek, perhaps mercifully, died out a generation or so ago. But not ledge walking.

"Just grab a root," my guide said, "and you'll make it across, no problem." Whereupon he grabbed a root himself. Right away it broke off in his hand.

"Wrong root," he grinned. Then he grabbed another root and

still another until at last he made it across the ledge. He gestured for me to do the same thing.

Look on the bright side, I tried to tell myself: If you plunge down the cliff face, at least you'll be avoiding all those arduous handholds and footholds on the way back. So I called up a double dose of adrenaline, grabbed a root, and stepped onto the ledge. All at once I seemed to be floating through the air, floating breezily, even lightheartedly, as if I'd been hoisted aloft by one of the island's tutelary spirits. A tutelary spirit, I might add, with a sense of humor. For when I returned to earth, I was standing on the opposite side of the ledge, grinning myself.

"All right?" my guide asked.

"Never felt better," I said, gazing down, far down on the greenest, loveliest jungle I'd ever seen.

I was not the first *memwai* (foreigner; lit., "sneaky person") to be seduced by Pohnpei's curious, albeit sodden level of reality. Probably the first was some anonymous beachcomber, more or less sodden himself.

But the first documented memwai was an Irish sailor named James F. O'Connell, who was shipwrecked here around the year 1830. Upon his arrival O'Connell promptly danced a jig, an act which so amused Pohnpeians that they adopted him on the spot. He was tattooed lavishly (later he became the first tattoo artist in an American circus) and provided with a chief's fourteen-year-old daughter as a wife. The only blot on this marriage seems to have been his wife Liauni's personal hygiene; she ate dog so often that she developed a virulent case of canine breath.

Shortly after O'Connell left, British and American whalers began putting in at Pohnpei for water and provisions. The island beckoned to them like the Promised Land. In 1843, the whaling ship

Fortune had to raise anchor with only four men before the mast; the rest had deserted. The *Offey* couldn't even raise anchor because it lost so many hands to desertion. Some of these deserters were nothing if not ingenious; one man even attempted to paddle ashore in his captain's bathtub. Then there was Captain John Eldridge, whose ship the *Harvest* was sunk by the Confederate raider *Shenandoah* in 1865. Rather than return home in disgrace, Captain Eldridge stayed on Pohnpei and went native.

As for the natives themselves, they often seemed to go whaler. Half-naked Pohnpeians would greet newly arrived missionaries with lines like: "Hullo, Jack. Will you give us a chew of 'baccy?" And like hard-bitten whalers, they tended to be indifferent to Christian doctrine as it was purveyed by these new arrivals. One early missionary, in fifteen years of the Lord's work, managed only a single convert—a retarded adolescent girl. Such men often ended up becoming traders, a profession equally unrewarding. For Pohnpeians would take them aside and tell them in a chummy voice: "A fine bloke like you, guess I can fix you up with two, three chicken— 'bout twenty dollar apiece—eh, Jack?"

The Pohnpeian identity remained more or less uninfluenced by these early contacts. Even successive colonial regimes, first Spanish (1886–1899), then German (1899–1918), Japanese (1918–1945), and finally American (1945–1986), seemed to have little effect on it except to give it a scattering of fresh genes.

And today, although Pohnpei has direct air connections with Guam, the most developed, most Americanized island in the Western Pacific, it remains resolutely traditional. Pohnpeian faces may look like advertisements for the Family of Man, with their Prussian jaws, Japanese cheekbones, and Melanesian skin color. Yet however cosmopolitan the faces, more than likely their possessors will be chewing *pwuh* (betelnut), drinking *sakau,* eating *mwuroi* (pigeon), or laid up with *sownmwaw-n-nan-yak,* a disease which features an inordinate passion for mangrove crab.

Speaking of inordinate passions, there's one that I consider more typically Pohnpeian than all the rest. Remember the water shortage that mystified me? I finally found out what caused it: Pohnpeians like the sound of water so much that they tend to leave their faucets running simply to listen to it.

———➤◆◄———

Quietly falls the shadow of night on Pohnpei, quietly and almost imperceptibly, except for one thing: the constant *plonk! plonk! plonk!* of stones pulverizing the roots of the sakau plant. Once pulverized, these roots are wrapped in hibiscus fiber and their juices squeezed into coconut shell cups, along with, occasionally, dirt, sweat, and spittle.

It's been said that the drinking of this concoction puts Pohnpeians in touch with their ancient gods. But the encounter is, everyone seems to agree, a rough ride for the senses. In fact, one of the nineteenth-century whalers described sakau as "the worst smelling, most nauseous compound upon which a man ever attempted to get salubrious."

One evening I set out to get, if not exactly salubrious, at least a passing acquaintance with this heady potion. I walked down the steep hill from my hotel, then took a meandering, deeply potholed road into Awak village. As I walked along this road, I could hear the musical ripple of streams everywhere, together with the seemingly universal drip-drip-drip of wet foliage. It had rained an hour or so earlier. And now the air had a leafy, gourdlike aroma that restored a lost savor to my nostrils.

At last I came to a thatched, open-air house barely illuminated by a single light bulb. Inside, benches were arranged haphazardly around a circular slab of rock where a man, Gregorio, was pounding sakau root. *"Kaselehlia,"* Gregorio called out to me. "Welcome."

As I sat down on a bench, half a dozen sakau drinkers smiled at me in unison. Doubtless they were wondering what would happen when I, a memwai, got in touch with their ancient gods. They didn't have long to wait, for Gregorio immediately handed me a coconut shell cup.

"Sakau is so sacred that you can't look directly at it," he told me. "If you look at it, you'll die within a year."

"But I've already looked at it," I said. As, indeed, I had. It looked not unlike the primordial ooze I'd sloshed through the day before.

"Well, maybe you'll just go blind," he smiled.

Now I raised the cup to my lips and took a tentative sip. What I swallowed had the taste and consistency of the aforesaid ooze. It reminded me somewhat of kava, which is made from the same plant. And since I'd drunk kava to no ill effect on other Pacific islands, I raised the cup again and swallowed its entire contents.

Kava, no matter how much of it I drank, never left me with more than a polite buzz. Not so sakau, as I soon learned. For Pohnpeians harvest the plant, pound its roots, and drink the result all in the same day, thus keeping sakau's bioactive ingredients alive. Also, they tend to dilute the mash hardly at all, which is why the experience of drinking sakau often seems like an experience of eating it.

After the first cup, I felt languid. After the second, inert. And after the third, I knew why Pohnpeians say that sakau makes you fall up rather than down. For I was floating through the air. Next to me, although many feet below me, a man named Raymond was telling a story about the origin of sakau. Long, long ago (he said), the god Lukh instructed a mortal woman to bury skin from his friend Uitannar's heel in the ground. The woman did as she was told, and after a plant sprouted, some rats began nibbling at its roots. The rats became *pupuda* (roaring drunk). Soon human beings were becoming pupuda, too.

All I could do in response to Raymond's story was nod dumbly and try to focus my eyes on his face. But I kept focusing on his elbow. Or maybe it was my elbow. Or maybe Gregorio's.

It seemed a good idea to take my leave before I lost total command of my senses. So I stood up and stumbled Chaplin-like onto the road, where I raised my thumb in the time-honored gesture of the hitchhiker. But so sakau'd were my motor reflexes that the thumb kept flopping down in the time-honored gesture of a Roman emperor. It was just as well, since there were no cars anyway.

In his book *The Caroline Islands,* the English writer F. W. Christian describes the characteristic sakau stagger as follows: "... one leg struggles south, while the other is marching due north." That's exactly how I moved, stumbling and careening, teetering and tottering down the road. At one point I stepped into a pothole and seemed to sink into it as if into a bottomless pit. At another point my zigzagging launched me down an incline and into a ditch. There I lay, blissful, until a sudden onslaught of rain reminded me of my mission—to get back to my hotel.

How I got back to the hotel, through the village and up the hill, I'll never know for sure. Maybe I just staggered on until I finally managed to arrive there. But maybe another tutelary spirit came to my aid, or at least set my navigation straight. If that happened, I did in fact get in touch with a Pohnpeian god ... and a most salubrious god it was.

———•◦•———

And then I went to Nan Madol.

Instead of making the trip by speedboat, I decided on the slower, more laborious route overland. A speedboat seemed somehow inappropriate for a site a thousand years in the making. Also, I'd become so accustomed to ooze, primordial or otherwise, that I was a little concerned about being whisked over the sea—it might prove an unpleasant shock to my system.

With Rufino Mauricio, Pohnpei's resident archaeologist, I drove southeast from Kolonia to Temwen Island. On nearby Pehlenkitel Island we stopped to see a man named Cornelius. Since his property adjoined Nan Madol, we needed his permission before we sloshed through it. Cornelius raised his eyebrows slightly, which is the Pohnpeian way of saying yes, go ahead, slosh all you want.

Now we began walking toward the most celebrated ruin in the Western Pacific. In a few minutes, we passed a small, partially over-grown structure in the typical Nan Madol style, with six-sided basaltic columns stacked alternately lengthwise and crosswise in cribs. Pohnpeians are wary of structures like this, especially after night-fall, Rufino told me, for they believe that Nan Madol's spirits only need the cover of night to come alive again.

"What happens when these spirits come alive?" I asked.

"They speak in strange hushed voices that seem to come from the stones themselves," he said.

Right now the only voices I could hear belonged to a couple of lorikeets squawking overhead. Apart from that, there was a deep silence that seemed almost calculated, as if the jungle were waiting for us to pass before resuming its usual raucous chorus of noises.

Soon we were wading through a sucking, burbling section of the island's mangrove swamp. Rufino took off his sandals rather than lose them to the covetous mud. We slopped through this mud, stepped over an old sea wall, slopped through more mud, and suddenly we were there. In the Big City.

Although I'd visited other archaeological sites on Pohnpei, nothing prepared me for this: nearly a hundred man-made islets inter-sected by channels and squared off into city blocks. Each islet boasted a hulking grey-black mass of stones—a temple, a medical center, priests' quarters, a royal residence, and so on. On one islet, Idedh, Nan Madol's sacred eels had their dining room; priests placated them with frequent servings of turtle entrails and baked dog. Rufino pointed to another islet, Darong, where a two-ton sakau stone had been discovered. Pohnpeians consumed sakau as eagerly a thousand years ago as they do today, he said.

It was like a vision of another world; a world that had lived and died stone, and worshipped stone in-between. I could see why the site had inspired outrageous or fanciful explanations, why Erich von Däniken, for example, thought Nan Madol the work of space aliens. Or why some Pohnpeians attribute its construction to a dragon. Or why others say it was begun by two brothers, Olosihpa and Olosohpa, with a talent for making stones fly.

History itself attributes Nan Madol, at least in its most significant phase, to the rise of the Deleur dynasty around the year 1000. Under this dynasty, the site became an elaborate cultural and religious center, as well as a center for cruel and despotic behavior. One Deleur ruler, Raiplinwoko, kept Pohnpeians in a pen and fattened them for his table. Another named Sakon Mwei had an insatiable appetite for lice; no one was allowed to harvest lice from his own head unless he first brought the most succulent louse to court. Yet another Deleur reputedly set fire to his house and then himself upon discovering that his mother-in-law was a crocodile.

But it's far easier to make your charges give up their lice than to make them haul around multi-ton basaltic blocks. Whether Pohnpeians did this hauling voluntarily or were forced to do it, or indeed *how* they did it (rafts? ramps? magic?) are mysteries whose solutions are—to use a Pohnpeian phrase—"lost in the weeds."

Now we waded across a channel and came to the islet of Nan Douwas. Here the Deleurs made baked shellfish offerings to their gods. Here too they buried their highest-ranking dead—the most priestly of priests and chiefly of chiefs—in stolid masonry vaults. But I was less impressed by these vaults than by the enormous double-walled enclosure fortifying them. With its upward flare, it looked like a cross between a Japanese pagoda and a log cabin over which someone forgot to put a roof. I peered up at its carefully fitted columnar stones with a certain awe. And from a height of thirty feet they seemed to peer down on me with a certain hauteur. As if they were presiding over an eternal realm and I, a mere mortal, had no business here.

The Deleurs were long gone, overthrown in the seventeenth century (so the story goes) by a warrior named Isokelekel. But I couldn't help feeling their not necessarily benevolent presence on Nan Douwas. I imagined their eyes secretly studying me through chinks in the stones, perhaps evaluating my potential as cuisine. I heard voices too, and although these voices seemed to belong to lorikeets shrieking in the distance, could I really be certain? Thus I felt a sense of relief when Rufino and I left the islet.

Before heading back to Kolonia, we stopped at Cornelius's house again. Cornelius's elderly father was sitting on a pandamus mat in an attitude of stately repose. On a whim I asked him if he thought Nan Madol's stones could have flown to their present location from wherever they were quarried. He replied:

"Stones can't fly. But you can make them light and easy to carry with an *amahra* (magic spell). With the right amahra, you can make a very heavy object almost weightless. But as for stones flying, no, it's impossible."

———⟫◦⟪———

In Salapuk, Pohnpei's most isolated village, lies a stone even more venerable than the stones of Nan Madol. Legend has it that this stone was put down by a demigod, Sapkini, in the act of building Pohnpei itself. Stone after stone Sapkini and his fellow demigods put down, but Salapuk's stone was their first, indeed the island's first palpable object.

Before I left Pohnpei, I wanted to visit this legendary stone. So

I drove with a guide to the coastal village of Wenik. From there we trekked inland along a gutted and rutted road that soon became a gutted and rutted trail, then a completely flooded trail. Climbing a ridge, we walked into a curtain of fog whose color and density reminded me of béchamel sauce. It wasn't long before we lost the trail and began wandering around in an apparently endless labyrinth of banyan trees and sword-bladed pandamus. My guide was no help; due to a sakau hangover, he was lost in a fog himself.

At one point my guide and I became separated. When I shouted his name, he came running toward me with a worried look on his face. "Don't *ever* shout in the mountains," he told me sternly. "Sokeles are everywhere. If they hear you, it's bad. Very bad. They kidnap you, and you spend the rest of your life inside a banyan tree."

From then on, I spoke very, very softly.

When the fog lifted an hour or so later, we were standing right in the middle of Salapuk. Muddy paths led off in all directions to thatched houses and cook sheds. I saw a man trying to make an uncooperative water buffalo pull a travois laden with yams. Beside a stream, several women in bright flower-print dresses were whacking their laundry. One of them looked up and stared at me in open-mouthed wonder.

"Maybe she see only three, four memwai in her whole life," my guide said.

It was raining, of course. A man named Nahnsen Eldridge—a lineal descendant of Captain Eldridge of the *Harvest*—invited us to take shelter in his house. His wife handed us plates of water buffalo meat, presumably from a beast that had refused its burden of yams once too often.

As I ate, I asked Nahnsen if he could direct me to Salapuk's illustrious stone. He shook his head. The stone was far too important for that sort of casual viewing, he said. To see it, I first needed to get permission from the local *nahnmwarki* (chief).

"Okay. Can you introduce me to him?"

"Unfortunately, the nahnmwarki is away for the day."

"Couldn't some lesser dignitary give me permission?"

Nahnsen lowered his eyebrows, which is the Pohnpeian way of saying no, absolutely not, case closed. Then his wife wove me a consolation prize, a chaplet of hibiscus and jasmine flowers, and placed it on my head.

Oh well, I thought: no trip is complete unless it remains a little incomplete, with at least one stone left unturned or unvisited to lure the traveler back.

But there was a nearby point of interest which I did not want to leave unvisited. So after the rain let up, my guide and I left Salapuk and hiked down a precipitous slope, most of which required the usual handholds and footholds. At the bottom we walked through a bed of wild ginger that gave off a surprisingly pungent reek. Then we began wading along a stream whose green mossy rocks were slick as ice. At last we arrived at our destination—a veritable river plunging downward over a sheer rock wall, ever downward for several hundred feet into a limpid pool below. This was Sahwartik, Pohnpei's largest and mightiest waterfall.

As I gazed at Sahwartik, suddenly I felt possessed by an inordinate calm. Nothing in the world seemed to matter except the aqueous bounty in front of me, pulsing, roaring, and then submitting to oblivion in the pool. Nothing else seemed to exist, either. It was as if I'd been granted an audience with the essence of Pohnpei in all its liquid splendor.

FARTHEST CARIBBEAN

Between 1929 and 1936 the eccentric English archaeologist Frederick Mitchell-Hedges dug up the Bay Islands of Honduras. He was hoping to find artifacts that would support his theory about Atlantis: namely, that the Bay Islands are the very tip of that lost continent, the rest being submerged. With him on his yacht *Amigo* were the baroness and author Lady Richmond Brown, a one-legged captain named Frank Boynton, a one-eyed Mexican crewman, and a local man who was wanted for murder in four Central American countries. On occasion the cabin boy was a Bay Islander from Bonacca Town, Guanaja, named George Haylock.

Today George Haylock is nearly eighty, a man with white beetling brows and an ever-present cigar, which he stabs in the air for emphasis. I met him one morning in his combination grog-shop/bakery in Bonacca and asked him what he most remembered about the Mitchell-Hedges expeditions. Atlantean potsherds? The missing body parts of his colleagues? Or perhaps Mitchell-Hedges's use of an Aztec crystal skull, complete with detachable jawbone, as a sort of personal talisman?

None of these things, he said. What he most remembered was making tea. Mitchell-Hedges and Lady Brown—the wife of a baronet—had come back from a dig and immediately wanted their tea. The cook was sick, so he, George, had to brew it. At the time he had never brewed a single cup of tea, good, bad, or indifferent, in his life. Sipping her tea, Lady Brown declared:

"George, this is quite the best cup of tea I've ever had."

He fixed me with his cigar. "You see, it's there, always there in the blood. English blood. *English*, my friend."

"What's there?" I inquired.

"The ability to make tea, of course," he replied in the Devonshire lilt of his ancestors.

———

Geographically, the Bay Islands—Roatan, Utila, and Guanaja, along with several lesser satellites—are in the Caribbean, moored off the northern coast of Honduras. But they seem to suggest almost everywhere *but* the Caribbean. Their stilt houses, jungly interiors, and dugout canoes suggest the South Seas. Their household god is the hammock, universally esteemed, seldom vacated, which suggests the South Seas, too. On the other hand, the vibrant insect population—sandflies, mosquitoes, ticks, scorpions, centipedes, bluebottles, and something green-eyed and wingéd whose mandibles made cookie-cutter indentations on my flesh—would seem to have been imported from an African insectarium.

And then there's Bonacca: its canals and canal aromas make it feel like a Venice fetched to the tropics from distant Italy.

This jumble of affinities has a history which reveals itself like a kaleidoscope, now offering an Indian artifact, now a West Country lilt, and now an African herb cure for waning virility or kidney stones. It's a history that includes a motley of scoundrels and adventurers, starting with Columbus, who reputedly dropped anchor at Guanaja in 1502, only to be told by the Paya Indians to move his ship, since a rather more important vessel, one laden with mainland trade goods, was expected momentarily. The celebrated English pirate Henry Morgan was here. So were Dutch pirates, French pirates, and Spanish slavers. So was the American soldier of fortune William Walker, as well as another soldier of fortune, less well known but no less audacious, a Louisiana-born man named Lee Christmas—the latter took over Utila and made himself its head of state on January 1, 1911, in order, so he blithely put it, to celebrate the New Year.

Robinson Crusoe was here, too. At least that's what a Utila man, wholly serious, told me. Defoe's hero, he said, was actually a pirate who'd buried his treasure on Utila and didn't want anyone to know about it, so he concocted an elaborate fiction about resourcefulness and survival on an island off Chile. To prove his point, the man showed me the very spot in the sand where Crusoe found Friday's footprint ...

Of all influences, it is the English which dominates the Bay Islands. English is the language of choice, not Spanish, and shillings are still invoked even though the Honduran *lempira* is the medium of exchange. Scratch a local and more than likely you won't find a Caribbean islander, ardently anti-colonialist, but a self-proclaimed Englishman. Even if the person's name happens to be Jesus.

"I think of the Queen like I think of my own mother," Jésus Morales, a Roatan boat-builder, told me.

In the reign of an earlier queen, Queen Victoria, England claimed the Bay Islands as part of a protectorate that included today's Belize and the so-called Miskito Coast. It was a sad day for islanders when the Crown ceded their home ground to the Republic of Honduras. It still is a sad day, more than 130 years later. In Coxen's Hole, Roatan, I found myself talking with a fisherman whose face was a jumble of Anglo, African, and Hispanic features. On a whim, I asked him how he'd feel if the Crown reclaimed its former colony. He'd been gutting a fish. He put down both the fish and his gutting knife.

"Is it really going to happen?" he said with an eagerness that made his eyes sparkle.

———⋙•⋘———

I began my Bay Island sojourn on Roatan, a long, serrated island shaped not unlike a string bean. For all most visitors see of it, it could be shaped like a turnip or a floweret of broccoli, because most visitors come for its luminous underwater realm and seem to regard anything above water as taboo. Not being a diver, I appreciated this—it meant Roatan's terrestrial estate would be mine and mine alone. Isn't it every traveler's selfish dream to have a whole island to himself?

In Sandy Bay I hired a guide for a walk along the chain of hills, known as Roatan's Alps, which make up the island's spine. This guide's name was Butterfly. Until recently his name had been Maurice, but he changed it—a common Bay Island practice—in hopes of changing his luck. As Maurice, he'd been broke. As Butterfly, maybe he'd become a millionaire. When I failed to see the connection between millionaires and butterflies, he grinned: "Millionaires always be flittin' about, mon. Like butterflies. I long to flit about myself so's I can see de world." He grinned again when I asked him about bugs on our walk. "No problem, mon." Fateful words!

If Butterfly's name wasn't Butterfly, neither are Roatan's Alps really Alps. The tallest scrapes the sky at only 771 feet, an altitude I kept in mind as our path rose steeply upward, past a deforested area, into a jungle of epiphytes, lianas, and giant hardwoods. So worn-looking was this path that I wondered if it'd been originally trodden by the Paya, in the days before the Spanish sold them all into slavery. I also wondered if maybe a handful of Paya had escaped their Spanish persecutors by fleeing into the jungle, *this* jungle. Maybe, just maybe their descendants were hiding only a few feet away, squinting at us through the dense foliage there.

As I was looking for camouflaged Indians, it began to rain. Not a soft drizzly sort of rain, but a clamorous downpour that seemed a first cousin to an Asiatic monsoon. We took refuge under the spreading canopy of a hardwood. All at once my nostrils detected the scent of perfume. It was the *ylang ylang* tree next to us, Butterfly said, adding that its juices are used in the manufacture of Chanel No. 5.

"You mean they don't use a synthetic?" I asked.

"No synthetic smells this good, mon." Whereupon he pressed his nose against the tree and happily inhaled.

The rain persisted, so we had no choice but to persist, too. We sloshed up Difficulty Hill, then sloshed down by a different route. Much of the vegetation on this route, I noted, had prickles, thorns, spikes, or spurs. One tree, in fact, stabbed me. Butterfly called it a Shake My Hand Tree, so named because its thorns seem to reach out with malicious intent and lacerate the passerby. Once lacerated, twice cautious. Now I avoided a lancietta palm, whose trunk was lined with two-inch spikes, sharp as a surgeon's lancet, and a fuzzy vine whose name Butterfly didn't know but whose hooked spicules, he said, were capable of removing a square inch of flesh in a trice.

Back on the road I made a 100-lempira contribution to Butterfly's first million. Just before we parted, he suggested that I change *my* name ... to Spike.

That night I noticed something quite odd: my body looked like a pointillistic painting, late period, by Georges Seurat. Somehow, during the day, I'd stumbled on a nest of tiny red *garrapatas* (a.k.a. "war ticks"), and now they covered me from head to toe. Several hours with a tweezers got rid of them, but it was too late. I itched. Powerfully itched. Relentlessly itched. I couldn't write in my journal unless I paused every few seconds to scratch an ankle, an armpit, or a flank. Not surprisingly, my sentences were very short.

Next morning one of the divers at my hotel asked where I'd been the previous day.

"Insect Heaven," I replied, itching. Part of me wished I'd been underwater with him, ogling angelfish, Nassau groupers, and eagle rays, none of which affix themselves to the visitor or impale him on their thorns. The other part, however, was pleased as punch to have made contact—direct bodily contact—with Roatan.

<hr />

Contrary to my imagination, there aren't any Paya Indians left on Roatan. But there are Garifuna, a people of mingled Carib Indian and African roots. Natives of St. Vincent, they'd refused to be penned up in reservations there. In 1797 the British rounded them up and deported them to the former pirate stronghold of Port Royal on Roatan. Most Garifuna couldn't tolerate Port Royal—a derelict shut-in place, with no cohune fronds for their roof thatch—and settled on the Honduran mainland. But a remnant stayed on at the northern fastness of Punta Gorda.

"There's absolutely nothing to see in Punta Gorda," a longtime American visitor to the Bay Islands told me.

High praise, indeed. I decided to go there and savor this absolute nothingness.

It was still raining when I took a bus with a terminal rattle from Sandy Bay to Oak Ridge. The rain had joined up with gusty winds—a "norther," Radio Belize said—by the time I started walking the road from Oak Ridge to Punta Gorda. Road is perhaps an exaggeration for what was simply a pair of ruts filled with reservoirs of water. After an hour these ruts dipped abruptly and some mud-and-wattle houses appeared, along with a couple of breeze block bungalows. Then I came to the village itself, which was sprawled along the shore for almost a mile. Its chief architectural feature was a long procession of outhouses, each perched at the end of a wooden plankway over the sea.

Down by the beach I watched a man hollow out a canoe from a single cedar log. He was wearing long, remarkably clean trousers and a John Deere cap, nothing else. His skin was a rich coppery-black. I greeted him with the only words of Garifuna I knew: *"Ida biangi?"* (How are you?)

He answered in a barrage of English, Spanish, and Garifuna, of which I understood only one word—"wet." I switched to English and asked whether there was anyone in Punta Gorda who knew about old Garifuna traditions.

"Ah, Grandpa Antonio," he said. And he took me to a simple thatched hut where a wizened old man lay in bed, seemingly feeble. We talked, or tried to talk. I mentioned a Carib story about the moon falling in love with an earthly woman and got only a blank stare. Then I mentioned my garrapata bites. Did he know any herb, decoction, or remedy to relieve the itching. He was silent for a moment, then said: "Get ... a ... cortisone ... shot."

Later I was sitting with the proprietor of the village snack bar. He'd heard the story of the moon's amorous liaison with the earthly woman, who, he said, became pregnant and eventually gave birth to a little moon. Speaking of which, the Garifuna used to think that a pregnant woman's eyes could burn up the vegetables in a garden. Also, they thought that a *buwiye* (shaman) could take a vine and turn it into a poisonous snake or take a poisonous snake and turn it into a harmless vine.

"But nobody believes in these superstitions anymore," the man said. "The Garifuna of today are more or less modern in the way they look at things."

"You speak English very well," I told him.

"I should hope so. I lived for twenty-five years in Brooklyn, New York."

And then he went on to lament the fate of the Dodgers after they forsook Brooklyn for the alien shores of California.

⎯⎯►•◄⎯⎯

Paradisiacal islands share a travel-poster sameness: the same untrodden beaches, the same palm trees fluttering gently in the trades, the same turquoise waters, and the same dusky maidens gaily bedecked with local flora.

Southwest of Roatan lies Utila, which seems to have been designed as an alternative to Paradise. It is low-lying and scruffy, even ugly by travel poster standards. The maidens are not dusky and the flora, much of it, wields the usual assortment of spikes and spines—very, very unbedeckable. Hordes of sandflies have squatter's rights to the beaches. And over half the island is taken up by a thick, almost impenetrable mangrove swamp. The only person known to have lived in this swampy part of the island was a nineteenth-century French hermit named Monsieur Baptiste, who had a passion for mangrove oysters.

Unlike Paradise, Utila is quirky. Imagine gingerbread stilt houses with sash windows and deep eaves, white picket fences and neatly trimmed bougainvillea, men idly chatting in the town square like bucolic English villagers, and the village idiot seated on a bench in this same square, muttering contentedly to himself, "The Lord loves me, the Lord loves me, the Lord loves me ..." Imagine, too, one of these bucolic villagers addressing you in the voice of a Wodehouse toff: "And how is Mr. Churchill doing these days? Getting a bit long in the tooth, I should think, the old bulldog."

Granted, Utila is hardly on the cutting edge of international reportage. And this particular fellow was a bit long in the tooth himself. Yet the island occupies such an airy plane of sensibility that one can envision Winston Churchill alive and well here even though he's dead everywhere else.

Item: a relict white population which, rather than going to seed in the tropics, has seeded itself enduringly there.

Item: a man who showed me the well he excavated upon receiving precise instructions ("Dig a little to the north, now a little to the east, *there*") from an angel.

Item: a cave, Brandon Hill Cave, reputedly used by both Henry Morgan and Robinson Crusoe.

Item: the words "Utilla Towne Garbigge Dumpe" painted with careful attention to lettering on a sign near the island dump.

One day I saw a Honduran gendarme with an M-14 slung over his shoulder and a book stuck in his back pocket. The rifle didn't surprise me, but the book did—Latin American policemen tend not to be very literary. As unobtrusively as possible, I followed him until he paused to check his timepiece in front of the Bucket of Blood Bar. Now I caught the title of his book —Garcia Marquez' *One Hundred Years of Solitude.*

This seemed a perfect title for an island as slow on the uptake, and as agreeably bygone, as Utila.

———⊳•◁———

On Utila I managed a couple of brief swims off my hotel's dock, but I refused any more intimate contact with the sea. It was still raining—another "norther," according to Radio Belize—and I figured that if I suffered any more moisture, I might warp or possibly rust. So I hung around the town square like a bucolic villager myself. Most of my companions were fishermen considerably displeased with the weather. Half playfully but also half in earnest, they blamed it on me, a visitor from the North who'd brought this succession of storms down with him.

To change the subject, I asked if anyone knew stories about the American adventurer Lee Christmas.

"Why, you can talk to Lee Christmas himself," was the reply.

"He lives here."

I took this statement to be of a piece with Winston Churchill's dogged survival on Utila. For if Lee Christmas were alive today, decrepit or not, he'd be at least 130 years old. Then I got to thinking: the richly patinated gravestones in the island cemetery did show that extreme old age has plenty of exemplars here ...

The Lee Christmas I met turned out to be a thin sturdy man of late middle years, scarcely a centenarian. He'd been born a Bodden, but his grandmother was so delighted by his namesake's seizure of Utila from the Hondurans that she went down to the local registry office and changed the boy's name to Lee Christmas.

"Lee Christmas was a tall, very handsome man," the present Lee Christmas said of his namesake, "and when he walked around the island in his cream-colored suit, all heads turned. Especially women's heads. He was King of Utila for about a week. And every day he climbed up Pumpkin Hill to see if a Honduran gunboat was coming to get him."

The rain had diminished to a drizzle, so I decided to climb Pumpkin Hill myself. I set out across The Bamboo—Utila's major pre-Columbian residential district—and soon found myself ankle-deep in mud and pottery shards. At last I reached the base of the hill, from which ten minutes of bushwhacking brought me to the summit. There I witnessed an extraordinary sight—not a Honduran gunboat belatedly coming to take back the island, not even a particularly photogenic view, but a bright ribbon of sunlight on the horizon. Above me glowering rain clouds were beating out a retreat like the powers of darkness before a superior deity.

But the appearance of the sun is not what I'll remember about that day. What I'll remember is this: I was walking back to the Bucket of Blood for a measure of brew when I noticed an elderly woman wearing a black high-collared dress and an antiquated frilly bonnet. She was seated in a chair on her verandah, rocking slowly back and forth, back and forth, perhaps dreaming of a childhood long ago, perhaps of England's green and pleasant land. She looked exactly like Whistler's Mother.

———◦◦◦◦———

From Utila I flew to La Ceiba on the Honduran mainland, then caught a DC-3 for the hop to the most northern of the Bay Islands—Guanaja. The plane seemed to be searching out a nonexistent runway before it suddenly touched down with a rollicking thump on a short strip of tarmac, braking at water's edge. Three people and one pig were awaiting its arrival.

Easternmost of the Bay Islands, Guanaja is actually two very different places: a piney mainland crumpled with hills, and Bonacca Town, also called Low Cay. The mainland is like a chunk of Polynesia crossbred with the Maine woods, whereas Bonacca consists of two small islands, Hog Cay and Sheen Cay, flat as pieplates and joined by landfill.

The first thing I did in Bonacca was pay a visit to the local doctor. In his surgery, I bared my posterior and he administered the cortisone shot prescribed by Grandpa Antonio. "It's a little too crowded here," he remarked.

He didn't mean my tick bites, likewise rather crowded, but Bonacca itself, a teeming, noisy hodgepodge of buildings flung together as if in an enormous hurry by a visually impaired town planner. The volleyball court seemed to occupy the confectioner's shop; the confectioner was nearly on top of the bridal shop; and the bridal shop had insinuated itself into the groggery next door. By all rights a five-minute walk in any direction should bring the walker to the sea. But the town is such a labyrinth of narrow streets, bridges, and canals that it will probably bring him right back to his point of embarkation ... in my case, the doctor's surgery.

Bonacca *is* too crowded, but it's so pleasantly rundown that it didn't make me think of the ghettoes of São Paolo or Hong Kong's Mong Kok district—it made me think of, well, the movies. The town could have been the setting for a Gable–Lombard romp in the South China Seas, circa 1935. Or it could have been where Joan Crawford went about being naughty in *Rain*.

Only in the movies would stilt houses rise a mere foot or so above the lapping sea, as many of them do here. If this were the real world, they'd be fodder for a hurricane, even a modest hurricane, or for a particularly aggressive spring tide. In fact, I mentioned this to a Bonacca householder. He answered my concern with a wry smile: "We rebuild a lot, mon."

The Guanaja mainland, on the other hand, is not crowded at all. Apart from the Lilliputian villages of Savannah Bight, Mangrove Bight, and Northeast Bight, it's empty—of people, that is. One afternoon I was walking along a coniferous ridge (Columbus called Guanaja, appropriately, "The Isle of Pines") when I heard voices. These voices were discussing me, I was convinced, and none too favorably, either. Then I gazed up. A couple of yellow-headed parrots were babbling away in a nearby treetop, with little or no regard for me, not even paying me the courtesy of an outraged squawk at my invasion of their territory.

And yet once upon a time there was quite a large population here. The slopes of Marble Hill, a 150-foot pinnacle a mile outside Savannah Bight, are so littered with Indian artifacts that I could close my eyes, bend down, and pick up a pottery fragment or a stone bead. In one crevasse I found part of an obsidian knife and a scattering of human teeth. In another, I found a so-called *yaba ding ding*—a pot leg with an incised human face. The yaba ding ding happened to be lying right next to an extended family of scorpions: black females carrying their tiny offspring, red males with yellow legs, still others bluish in color, gender indeterminate.

I interpreted this as an obvious sign not to disturb the yaba ding ding. With its perpetually staring eyes and oval mouth, it was Guanaja's, not mine. Best to leave it in its rightful resting place—to remind future visitors that they are not the first, nor will they be the last, to pass this way.

Also, I did not want any further dealings with insects.

<hr>

In Guanaja the sun became the blazing orb of tropical legend, so I finally decided to take the plunge. Donning snorkel and flippers, I waded out from El Soldado Beach, where Columbus anchored, to the fringe of the world's second largest barrier reef.

Nile green and crystal clear, the water was like a conjuror's cape, out of which I felt anything, *anything*, might materialize. Perhaps I'd discover a Columbian artifact, the coral-encrusted barrel of a harquebus, say, or a European bauble traded to the Indians and thrown away in disgust by them. Or perhaps I'd find evidence— the barely visible remains of a sunken city?—that would confirm the Mitchell-Hedges theory about the Bay Islands being Atlantis.

And I did find a sunken city, a thriving one, too. A school of yellowtail snappers hurried by like commuters at rush hour; rainbow parrotfish were nibbling the algae off coral with audible rasps; a trio of eagle rays fluttered past me in squadron formation; trumpetfish hung upside down as if their sense of balance were completely awry; anemones opened and closed their pink-tipped tentacles; and a fiercely territorial damselfish parried and thrust at intruders several times its size. At one point I saw a large green moray, its viperous mouth stuck in a maniacal grin, and wondered what it would look like with earrings (wealthy Roman ladies used to put earrings on their pet morays).

At another point I noticed a dark shape moving ominously in my direction. The word "shark" jolted me out of my reverie. Yet this shark seemed to be moving along the surface, slowly, almost painfully, so I thought "sick shark" and felt somewhat less apprehensive. I felt even less apprehensive when I lifted my head out of the water and saw that the dark shape was a dugout canoe.

I waved.

The man in the canoe waved.

Then he went back to paddling his ancient craft, I to my study of parrotfish and anemones, and the next time I looked up, he was a distant dot. Meanwhile, the sea had turned a deep turquoise, the color of—dare I say it?—Paradise.

POLYNESIA'S LAST
STRONGHOLD

❧

It was the rainy season in Western Samoa and yet I hadn't encountered any rain at all, only the bright South Pacific sun, an orb so intense that it turned these islands into a palm-clad blast furnace. Even Samoans were bothered by the heat. They'd spend long hours submerged in the sea, their brown heads like flotillas of coconuts rising and sinking with each wave, never quite ready to make a landfall.

Then one day the sky clouded over. And as if to compensate for the previous lack of moisture, suddenly a mighty grist of rain began clamoring down from the sky. I took refuge under an empty *fale,* opened my notebook and wrote: "The monsoons have arrived with a locomotive roar."

Locomotive roar? A wholly inappropriate word, I thought, for islands so resolutely unmodern. The nearest thing to a locomotive in Samoa is the native-style bus, a rickety open-air contraption, gaudily painted and more or less medieval in origin. So I crossed out "locomotive" and wrote "monumental." No good, either. For my notes already abounded with this word, usually invoked to describe the Samoan physique—male and female, young and old, almost every Samoan I'd met seemed to be built along the lines of a NFL linebacker.

Now I rewrote the sentence: "A tropical downpour has put Samoa in a rare Conradian mood." But I crossed out "rare," too. I planned to use that word to describe the *manumea* (*Didunculus strigirostris*), a strange and indeed rare bird whose taxonomic position is unclear. Could it be the last living relation of the dodo? The American naturalist Titian Peale thought so. Others put this toothbilled, purple-headed avian somewhere on the periphery of the pigeon family.

All at once I noticed a young girl had joined me in the fale. Swathed in a paisley-patterned *lavalava,* she was gazing at me with wide, intent eyes.

"What you do with paper?" she asked.

"I'm writing up the day's adventures," I said.

"But why you tear up day's adventures?"

"Because my mot juste is missing, probably drowned in this rain."

"Hah. You funny *palagi*. Are you married? Have husband?"

"No. And I don't have a wife, either."

By now virtually every child for miles around had joined us in the fale. They touched me, examined my effects, even studied the torn-up scraps from my notebook as if they were studying the fragments of a long-lost palimpsest. All the while they kept shouting: "Palagi! Palagi!"

I averaged thirty or forty "palagis" a day, more in remote villages, fewer in Apia, the country's capital. The word means Sky Burster and derives from the fact that the first foreigners to fetch up on these shores seemed to have burst forth from the sky itself. I liked being called a palagi—the word made me feel instantly transcendental, as if my place of residence was in fact the sky.

I would shout back at palagi-hurlers: "Sacred Chicken! Sacred Chicken!" For Samoa's name (*sa:* sacred, *moa:* chicken) memorializes a pair of chickens owned by Lu, son-in-law of the god Tagaloa, creator of all things. Unfortunately, the birds were eaten. But their memory survives to this day on every map of the world.

So there I sat, a transient from the upper atmosphere, until the rain passed. Then the children left me to my scribbling. It mattered not that one of them, so sweet, so innocent, had picked my pocket. After all, he or she only took the balloons that I was going to hand out anyway. And later that afternoon the theft granted me this vision: a solitary blue balloon moving slowly with the wind, past a stretch of greensward, past a row of thatched fales, past the bobbing heads of Samoans in the sea, then venturing out to the ordinary world beyond.

⸺◆⸺

Western Samoa should not be mistaken for its neighbor, American Samoa, on whose Ta'u Island Margaret Mead did the fieldwork for her now controversial book *Coming of Age in Samoa*. Even so, red-blooded male tourists occasionally show up at the Western Samoa Visitors Bureau waving Mead's book and wanting to find free-spirited adolescent girls like the ones depicted in its pages.

Nor should it be mistaken for those user-friendly Polynesian destinations where the visitor sprawls all day on a beach and by night watches immemorial customs enacted beside his hotel pool. To sprawl on a Western Samoan beach, it's often necessary to get permission from a village *matai* (chief), a process so potentially time-consuming that it can preclude the sprawl itself. As for customs enacted beside hotel pools, at least one—the famous fire dance—was introduced not so long ago by Mormon missionaries who thought it would be a hit with tourists (they were right).

It is the other customs, less immediately crowd-pleasing, that make Western Samoa the most fervently traditional of South Seas places. The full-body tattoos, the blowing of triton shells, the use of mats to determine wealth, the bird and beetle harbingers of death—they sustain a way of life that often seems to reach back, far back, to the time of Tagaloa himself. Consider the *liutofaga* or "shifting of bones" ceremony. An ancestor's bones are dug up, lovingly anointed with coconut oil, and then given pride of place in one's fale. A bit ghoulish, I dare say, for re-enactment beside a hotel pool. But it identifies a prominent feature of Samoan culture: past and present occupy a simultaneous realm, magically inseparable.

A closely-knit geography unusual for the Pacific helps keep this culture intact. For unlike Fiji, Tonga, or the Cook Islands, Western Samoa is not an archipelago of mostly flyspeck islets scattered over hundreds of miles of empty ocean. It consists of two very large islands, Upolu and Savai'i, separated by a 13-mile channel in which two small islands, Manono and Apolima, rest like stepping stones. This creates a united front so uncompromising that it can absorb or not absorb outlandish Sky Burster influences as it sees fit. And if absorbed, such influences become automatic Samoan property—delightfully, often outlandishly so.

Take Samoan cricket, for instance. The game, first introduced in 1885 by the officers and crew of the H.M.S. *Diamond,* is played in Samoa as one imagines cricket might be played in a surrealist dream. The bat is three-sided and resembles a war club with the stabbing spike knocked off. Any ball that comes into contact with it tends to move in mysterious ways, often ending up in churches, outhouses, or the sea. Roads are utilized as cricket pitches; the batting team has a distinct advantage because the fielding team invariably must dodge passing vehicles. Since it's also an advantage to field more players than your opponent, a hundred or more people on a side is not uncommon—if your ancient granny is still limber, there she'll stand with war club in hand.

Cricket, I ought to add, is the country's national pastime.

Slightly more than 170,000 people inhabit the four islands of Western Samoa. By conservative estimate there are at least twice that many *aitus* (ghosts). Any individual who has never seen an aitu must be reckoned blind, deprived, or both.

Aitus, I was told, can appear day or night, on the roads, in the bush, even on cricket pitches. Perhaps in televisions, too—one man told me that he refused to own a TV for fear that an aitu might get inside it. Another man mentioned an aitu that had walked brazenly into his fale during evening prayers. Robert Louis Stevenson's aitu, everyone agreed, was harmless. All it ever did was wander around with pen and manuscript, trying to finish *Weir of Hermiston,* Stevenson's final incomplete novel. But other aitus could be rather troublesome, particularly if they felt slighted in some way by a living family member.

Yet I was told not to worry if I found myself possessed by an aitu: I could always drop in on a healer and undergo a simple procedure to have it exorcised. (Couldn't a person bring his possessed TV to a healer, too? I wondered.)

I didn't give this any more thought. Then one day I slipped on a muddy slope near Upolu's Lake Lanoto'o and landed with my entire weight on my wrist. An excruciating jab of pain shot up to my shoulder, migrated back to the wrist, and then seemed to permeate the entire arm. So great was this pain that I found I couldn't even hold my pen in order to write up the day's adventures. Damn, I thought, there goes the trip. But a Samoan friend came to my aid. That night he took me to see an old woman, a healer, who lived a couple of miles outside Apia. Her surgery was a single shelf of vials and bottles with dubious-looking herbs floating inside them.

"I think something might be broken," I told the woman.

"Maybe," she said, "but you also have aitu problems."

She proceeded to rub some sort of herbal concoction up and down my arm, then skittered her fingers over it, alternately kneading and smooth ng the skin. As she was doing this, she closed her eyes and began muttering an incantation which the early missionaries doubtless would have frowned upon. After half an hour she said: "Arm all right now."

And indeed the pain had vanished, vanished entirely. When I looked to her for an explanation, she merely gave me an enigmatic smile, as if to say: There are more things in heaven and earth, Sky Burster, than are dreamed of in your philosophy.

——➤◆◄——

Robert Louis Stevenson, in a sense, had always been an aitu. At least his corporeal self always seemed pale, weedy, and likely to evanesce at the slightest provocation. In 1889 he arrived in Western Samoa in search of a final refuge from the cold rains of his native Scotland. The next year he built his estate Vailima on 400 lushly forested acres behind Apia. And there, in a sort of tattered splendor, he spent the last four years of his short life with his wife Fanny, her son Lloyd Osbourne, and an assortment of Samoan retainers bundled in lavalavas of Royal Stuart tartan.

The man Samoans called Tusitala (Storyteller) had an anticolonialist temperament not altogether common among nineteenth-century authors. He was so eager to see the land of his adoption free from foreign (German, British, and American) domination that he offered his pen to the cause of an independent Samoa. He also secured the release of some matai put behind barbed wire by the German authorities, a gesture which endeared him to his Samoan hosts. So it was that when he died in 1894—he suffered a fatal brain hemorrhage while making a salad dressing—several hundred Samoans hacked a path to the summit of Mount Vaea and passed along his frail remains to their final resting place 1,300 feet above the sea.

I had always wanted to visit Stevenson's grave and pay homage to a writer whose books had redeemed so many boring childhoods, perhaps so many boring adulthoods, too. So I chose an atypically cool day and climbed Mount Vaea with a Samoan named Simi. Simi said he needed the exercise, but most of our exercise came from stepping over the convoluted hardwood roots that lay athwart the trail. Every once in a while we stopped and looked out over a distempered skyline of broken trees—evidence of 1990's Cyclone Ofa, called "The Storm of the Century" by Samoans until another cyclone just as bad came the following year.

As we were climbing, I asked Simi if he knew any story about Stevenson that had been passed down by word of mouth over the generations. He thought for a moment, looked down at some doubtful needlework on his lavalava, then said this:

"You saw the stream below Vailima? Tusitala used to spy on the girls bathing naked there. That's what my old grandmother told me. She was one of the girls."

At last we reached the summit, which boasted a superb view of Apia straggling along a coral-knobbed incurve of the blue Pacific. I couldn't help feeling a little disappointed by Stevenson's tomb, however. Not that I wanted something grandiose and bizarre, like Sir Richard Burton's marble Bedouin tent in London's Mortlake cemetery. But I was surprised that the author of *Treasure Island* lay beneath a nondescript block of grey cement and that his famous epitaph ("Home is the sailor, home from the sea ...") had been all but obliterated by time, weather, and graffiti. Although I took the requisite photographs, I could easily have been photographing any of the nondescript cement blocks under which Samoans put their own dead. Except for one significant difference: the Samoan dead tend to be buried in the front yard, where they'll feel right at home (literally) and where presumably they can be dug up at short notice. Stevenson, by his own choice, rests in this solitary place for all eternity.

The difference was not lost on Simi, who felt it was wrong for a person, distinguished or otherwise, to be at such a remove from family, friends, and village. That Stevenson's wife lay under the same slab only convinced him that husband and wife were both standoffish. It didn't matter that they were dead. Even the dead, in Samoa, have social obligations.

"It is very strange," Simi observed, "but you palagis always prefer to be alone ... like Ava Gardner."

"Greta Garbo," I corrected him. And I figured the subject was closed. But on the way down the mountain we began discussing our respective families and I happened to mention that my mother lived by herself. Simi was first astonished, then appalled. My own mother, flesh of my flesh, *alone?* Why, he would go to America and look after her himself ...

———※———

All around the Pacific I'd heard stories about the capacity of Samoans for violence on a heroic scale. Not only did they break limbs and crush skinnier races beneath their monumental bodies, but—according to a Tongan I once met—they still practiced a bit of headhunting even at this late date. So I prepared myself for the worst. If my head ended up adorning a Samoan mantel, at least it would be spared the burden of a tomb like Stevenson's. Yet, truth to tell, I didn't encounter any headhunting or even head bashing on my Samoan trip. During the one occasion when the latter might have occurred, a huge anti-government demonstration in Apia, there was only singing and general high spirits. I half expected to see this headline in the newspapers the next day: *Government Brought Down By Cheerfulness.*

In fact, Samoans struck me as being among the most unaffectedly kind, most hospitable people I'd ever met. Almost every time I entered a fale, someone would be appointed to fan my overheated body. In one fale an old man nearly burst into tears because I was his guest and he had nothing to feed me—eventually he offered me, with great ceremony, a stale Tootsie Roll. And then there was the little girl who treated me to a recitation of "Baa, Baa, Black Sheep" because she thought it would remind me, global wanderer that I was, of home. This last gesture touched my heart, although I wondered if she thought my home was a sheep fold.

But such hospitality can have a punishing effect on a traveler's best-laid plans. Let me illustrate.

In my birdwatcher's search for a manumea, I'd gone to Upolu's Aleipata district. I figured this would be as good a place as any to obtain a sighting of one of these rare birds. For manumeas nest primarily in the cyclone-free craters of extinct volcanoes, something which this district had in abundance.

It seemed a simple enough procedure: ask the local matai for permission to visit a couple of craters, even offer him a few *tala* for the privilege. So I looked around until I located the matai in question. He was squatted cross-legged on a mat in his fale, seemingly impervious to the hectic pulse-beat of the outside world. His fully tattooed body gave him a somewhat mythical appearance, half man and half reptile.

"Ah, the manumea," he said. "Please have some tea."

This I expected, since it's impossible to accomplish any task in Samoa without first submitting to the appropriate formalities. I squatted down on a mat myself, taking care not to point my legs at my host. To point one's legs at one's host is considered extremely rude, worse even than sneezing in his face.

After the matai's wife served us fish, taro root, and tea, we bowed our heads. The matai gave a speech in which he thanked the Almighty for our humble repast. I made a speech to the Almighty myself, albeit a silent one, in which I thanked Him for not including *pisupo* in the repast. Virtually the national food, pisupo is canned

LAWRENCE MILLMAN

corned beef that's short on beef and long, very long, on fat—hippo fat, it's said, as well as cow fat. Whenever I saw a gelatinous heap of it on my plate, I would find myself with unexpectedly fond thoughts of famine and starvation.

After we finished eating, the matai bowed his head again and offered another prayer. Then he looked at me. "They say the manumea is related to the dodo," he said.

Ah, the manumea. My exit cue, I thought. And not a moment too soon, for my back was killing me. As it always killed me whenever I had to sit bolt upright on a mat for any length of time. But just as I was getting ready to ease my body into a standing position, the matai offered me more tea. I smiled and said no, that I really had to leave now. Whereupon he too smiled and poured me another cup.

Two cups of tea and a drinking nut of coconut water later, I found I could excuse myself without making a serious breach of etiquette. Now the matai cleared his throat and launched into a speech wherein he extolled my virtue, my manliness, and my wondrous attributes as a guest. I would always be welcome in his village, he said, and particularly welcome if I returned some day with a brand-new Evinrude outboard motor.

The speech seemed to go on ... and on ... and on. When it was over, the matai's wife began a speech of her own in which my virtue was again extolled. I started to wonder whether I might end up spending the rest of my virtuous days on this mat, the bones of my spinal column slowly turning to liquid. Another headline, this one for my obituary, passed before my eyes: *Travel Writer Dies. Mat Mortality Syndrome Suspected As Cause.*

I left the matai just as daylight was fading gently through the feathered tops of palms outside his fale. And with it faded my chance to poke around any of Aleipata's craters. Back in my Apia hotel room I jotted these words in my notebook: "Manumea elusive— Samoan hospitality quite the opposite."

Open-handed and generous, Samoans are a people ideally suited to their own open-air fales. See, they seem to be saying, we have nothing at all to hide. Of course, they use mats like blinds and pull them down at night, but that's not so much for privacy as it is to keep out birds, insects, and apparently emancipated animals—it's quite unnerving to wake up in the middle of the night and discover a pig rooting around your bedroom.

And yet there's also a secret, mystic quality to Western Samoa— a hoarding of gifts, if you will—that often left my senses jumbled. Who, exactly, is the Sky Burster here? I'd ask myself. Certainly not me, for I felt as if I'd forsaken my earthly home for a divine else-where, a place where time had lost all its compulsion, even more a place with no context but its own otherworldliness.

Especially on Savai'i, the larger, more sparsely populated of the two main islands, the local numen seemed not entirely of this world. I would pass a group of women scrubbing a rock face with whisk brooms. How inordinately clean Samoans are! I'd think. And later I would learn that the women were catching *inganga,* an amphibi-ous, eminently edible fish for which a whisk broom is the perfect tackle. Or I'd see Old Faithful mysteriously transported to Taga village and then realize I was watching a fountain of seawater—a blowhole—rising up through a limestone vent. Or I'd be traveling down a road and a village would appear in front of me, then the road would switch back on itself and the village would recede to the horizon, its prospect as phantasmal as Oz.

Mere sleights-of-hand, easily accounted for, it's true. But what of the Pulemelei Mound? This enormous step pyramid, forty feet high and more than 200 feet long, is the largest man-made prehis-toric monument in Polynesia. When I saw it, at first it *appeared* unmysterious, with birds and butterflies flitting gaily about and a single errant pig standing on the top step like a sentinel. But appearances can be very deceptive. In fact, the mound has cast an all but inscrutable glance at archaeologists, historians, and Samoans themselves, none of whom can explain what it is doing in the middle of Nelson plantation, for what possibly esoteric purpose it was built and by what long-vanished civilization.

Then the pig stumbled down Pulemelei's overgrown steps, the sky abruptly clouded over, and I felt the mound's cryptic force myself: aloof and perhaps a little mocking, it seemed to be coaxing me into a dare. Go ahead, the dare said, heap clichés on me, brutal human sacrifices, moonlit funeral corteges, war canoes sighted from my lofty heights. Whatever you think, you'll be wrong.

A few days later I drove to a rocky promontory at Savai'i's westernmost tip and visited the most otherworldly spot of all—the entrance to the Other World itself. Here, according to tradition, recently disembodied souls plunge into the sea and are then taken by canoe to heaven or hell. It's said that you can hear these souls pass by en route to their Eternal Rewards.

My Samoan guide was not happy to be here. He pleaded with me to hurry up so we could see the giant footprint of the war-god Moso—*very* interesting, he kept repeating—a couple of miles down the road. I found this a sinister place too, yet I didn't want to leave it so soon after we arrived. So I walked inland a short distance and investigated the Vaisuatoto Blood Well (was that really blood at the bottom, or was it simply the island's red volcanic soil?), then climbed onto a mound similar to Pulemelei but much smaller. The mound had been more or less reclaimed by jungle, but I could still see pottery shards, tile, and pieces from an old kava bowl among its roots and leaves.

Stooping down to pick up a piece of pottery, I heard something whoosh loudly past my head. What, I wondered, was *that*? It couldn't have been a bird because Samoa doesn't have a bird the size of, say, a California condor. And besides, no bird would fly at such speed through such thick bush and so close to the ground, too. My guide was waiting back in the car, so he couldn't have made the sound unless he was a ventriloquist. Then what had made it? The more I asked myself this question, the more uneasy I became, until at last I decided that there were indeed more things in heaven and earth than I dreamed of.

———◦◦◦———

Before I left Western Samoa, I was still determined to catch a glimpse, however fleeting, of a manumea. Warren Jopling, an Australian geologist now living in Samoa, told me about a crater on Savai'i's Tafua Peninsula which reputedly had a mating pair. That afternoon we drove down to Tafua on a road that soon disintegrated into a pair of sandy arteries. In the back seat of Warren's van was a boy named Fialupe. Fialupe had the ability to imitate a manumea's mating call, an invaluable talent, Warren said, on a mission like this.

First we paid the obligatory call on the local matai, then we climbed up a steep path to the top of Mount Tafua. From there we peered down on a crater so classically craterlike—its lush jungle flora notwithstanding—that I expected it to erupt at any moment. And erupt it did: dozens of fruit bats suddenly took to the air and swarmed above us, so close that I could see their delicate foxlike faces quite clearly. The Samoan fruit bat is one of the few bats in the world that happily performs its airborne maneuvers in broad daylight.

Now Fialupe cupped his hands to his mouth and called out: "*Goo, goo, goo.*" We waited, but there was no answer. He made the call again, this time a little more plaintively. And again there was no answer. So he turned his attention to a mosquito on his arm and began wagging his finger around it. "I'm hypnotizing it," he said.

LAWRENCE MILLMAN

In ever-decreasing circles went the finger, until finally he squashed it. Even the killing of a mosquito, I thought, has a ceremonial aspect to it in these islands.

All at once I heard a nearly inaudible cry of *"goo, goo, goo"* from deep inside the crater. That was it, just the muffled three-note cry, and then silence. But this cry solved at least one of Samoa's mysteries to my satisfaction. Solved it, that is, until Warren said he wasn't certain that the cry had been made by a manumea. It could have been made by some other bird, perhaps even a common dove.

"It could have been made by a ghost, too."

Or so Fialupe remarked.

This last explanation seemed the most logical, in Western Samoa.

NORTHERN
OUTPOSTS

AT THE TOP OF
THE WORLD

In Iglulik, you'll see chunks of sea-ice that have been whittled into exquisite works of art by whipcrack winds and the sun's beams. You'll find perhaps the only school in the world named after a cannibal. You'll watch three-hour sunsets where day and night seem to have locked hands on the horizon. And you'll hear outdoor concerts with performers so dedicated that they'll bite you if you try to interrupt their music.

The village of Iglulik lies two hundred miles above the Arctic Circle in the northern reaches of Canada's Foxe Basin. To go there for the usual touristic reasons—sightseeing, multi-star restaurants, museums, and so on—would be like going to Saudi Arabia for the vintage Chablis. In fact, I asked a local Inuk how many tourists had shown up this year. None, he said. None the year before, either. Then he scratched his head and asked what exactly a tourist was.

This, I confess, delighted me. For every traveler dreams of having an entire destination to himself.

Yet Iglulik isn't every traveler's dream destination. For one thing, it's situated on an island so barren that even the stoniest outposts of the Maine coast seem like veritable jungles by comparison. This island is not scenic, at least not conventionally so, being flat as a pancake or indeed flat as the pack-ice that surrounds it much of the year.

Then, of course, there's the climate—nine-month winters followed by a somewhat milder spell which passes for the other three seasons. Even during this so-called mild spell, winds can be so fierce that telephone and electrical poles must be anchored in big pots of stone or else they'd be picked up and flung bodily into Foxe Basin.

And yet this hard-edged chunk of arctic geography has a singular beauty of its own. To walk on its gravelly scurf is to become one with the ancient bedrock of the continent. And to see a lone immaculate arctic poppy peering forth from this same scurf is to witness an unsung act of heroism. For whatever grows at latitude 70°N does so of its own volition, with hardly a nudge from Mother Earth.

Equally singular are Iglulik's outdoor concerts, which take place every night, regardless of weather. The musicians are without exception off-duty sled dogs. One of them will start off by howling a long intricate riff in bass-baritone, alto, or choir-boy soprano. Then all the others will join in, one by one, until the whole village is howling.

Most of the time I'd find this music quite exhilarating. But occasionally, when the performers got carried away in the pursuit of their art, it would seem both loud and endless if not downright maddening. And one evening, when it was even louder and more endless than usual, I grabbed my sleeping bag and trekked over several miles of early Paleozoic limestone to the other side of the island, there, hopefully, to sleep.

After a mile or so, eager for a bit of non-canine music, I switched on my Walkman. But the only thing I could hear was a very distant crackling. Iglulik, it seemed, was too isolated to pick up any radio waves except those emitted by its own station. And that station recently had gone bankrupt when someone used its telephone to rack up $1,100 worth of calls to recorded sex messages in southern Canada.

Yet despite such incidents, Iglulik remains a bastion of Inuit traditionality. Its inhabitants still hunt for their food on land or sea rather than in a supermarket. Also, most seem to prefer the rough comforts of a tent on the tundra to the more obvious comforts of a modern bungalow in the village. So when I arrived at the other side of the island, I wasn't surprised to find several large white tents pitched there.

Smiles greeted me right away, along with querulous looks. Why was I carrying a sleeping bag around with me? I did an imitation of a howling sled dog with an imaginary knife suddenly drawn across its throat. An elderly couple thought this so hilarious that they gestured me over to their tent. The man was small and barrel-chested, as was his wife. Both looked like lead actors in a remake of *Nanook of the North*.

Said the man: "You sleep with us in tent tonight." Then he added: "We have you for dinner, too."

Were it not for the man's lack of ease with English, I would have been rather concerned about this last statement. For the Inuit are no strangers to the practice of having each other for dinner— quite literally so. Almost everyone in Iglulik has parents or grand-parents who avoided starvation by eating human flesh. Attagutaluk School, in fact, is named for a woman who ate the bodies of her dead family, although it was probably her later role as a commu-nity leader more than her act of cannibalism that led to this honor.

Now the man and woman piled food in front of me, more food than I could possibly eat in a single sitting. Mercifully, they didn't offer me such delicacies as *tugtup kumait* (warble fly larvae), *ipsanaq* (the stomach contents of walrus), or caribou brain au naturel. But they did offer me something that met my gaze with a distinctly unhappy gaze of its own.

"Eye of seal," the man said. "Very good. Tastes like egg. Inuit people like eye of seal very much."

"You ever cook it?" I inquired.

"Inuit people don't like cooked. Much better this way."

Whereupon he took a bite from it and smiled approvingly.

I looked away. As perhaps my host himself would have done if I had taken a bite from an asparagus, an eggplant, or a cauliflower. For one culture's seal eye is another culture's poison. Consider an incident that took place shortly after Iglulik's first contact with *qallunaat* (white people; lit., "those who pamper their eyebrows"). This initial contact occured in the year 1822, when a British Navy expedition, under Captains W.E. Parry and G.F. Lyon, wintered over here en route to not finding the Northwest Passage.

One day a group of Captain Lyon's sailors found a woman all alone in an ice-house. Too old to do any work, she'd been left there to starve. The kindly sailors took pity on her and offered her ship's biscuit, jam, salt pork, and sweets. She smiled in gratitude and pretended to nibble at what they'd given her. But when the sailors weren't looking, she threw it all away. Starvation, it would appear, was preferable to Royal Navy rations.

My hosts were seated right beside me, so I couldn't very well throw away the seal eye. But I couldn't bring myself to eat it, either. Instead, I put it aside and dined on boiled walrus, brisket of seal, and bannock, fare that seemed to me slightly less disturbing. At one point I noticed a couple of stray caribou hairs floating around in my tea. No matter: I merely plucked them out and flicked them away. Yes, my hosts' grins seemed to say, we too find caribou hairs somewhat unpalatable.

A while later I adjourned to their tent. It was crowded with grandchildren and slightly aromatic, not to mention being a bit draughty. Even so, I slept the sleep of the blessed.

Having dined on walrus, I now decided to view the animal in

LAWRENCE MILLMAN

its nonculinary aspect. So the very next day a man named Markassie took me to a walrus haul-out site in his motor-boat. Because of its relative proximity to the floe-edge, Iglulik is closer to such sites than any other village in the Arctic.

Weatherwise, this day could not have been more perfect. Beams of high latitude sunlight made the temperature seem almost warm. There was virtually no wind, with the result that the sea had a calm pink-pearly sheen to it … except when pieces of floating ice gave it an equally calm white sheen.

Likewise the air was of such exceptional clarity that I could see the mountains of Baffin Island fifty miles away; with each shift of the sun's position in the sky, they'd put on a whole new set of colors, turning now buff, now magenta, and now a rich shade of blue.

So perfect was this day that I could not imagine myself wanting to be anywhere else. Not in the shirtless tropics, and certainly not on some oppressively hot, overcrowded Mediterranean beach. And as I was gazing out, an ivory gull flew past the boat. This rare, all-white bird was like an exclamation mark punctuating my geographical prejudice.

Markassie had a good command of English, so I asked him his opinion of Nunavut. Nunavut, which means "Our Land" in Inuktitut, refers to the new Inuit-governed territory recently created from central and eastern sections of Canada's Northwest Territories. Covering a fifth of the country's 4,000,000 square miles, it will become official as of April 1, 1999. Iglulik, located squarely in the middle of this new territory, is one of the candidates being considered for its legislative capital.

"Some people think Nunavut is a good thing," said Markassie. "Myself, I am not so sure. We Inuit are hunters, not office workers. And Nunavut will put so many of us into offices that our culture may disappear as a result…"

This prompted Markassie to ask me a question. He was a little confounded by White Man's idea of Heaven, he said. It seemed to him odd that anyone would want to give up drinking, smoking, carousing, and bad language for—what?—a pair of wings. He wondered if I, a seemingly intelligent qallunaaq, would suffer such privation for so paltry a reward.

Before I could answer him, I heard a noise that sounded simultaneously like the roaring of a bull, the barking of a dog, and the neighing of a horse. Off to our starboard was the floe-edge, and on it lay a dozen or so paunchy, vastly overweight bodies in an attitude of stately repose. Even at several hundred feet I could see their downcurved ivory tusks gleaming brilliantly in the sunlight. As we eased closer, I began to see their spiky whiskers and Colonel Blimp jowls, too.

"*Aiviq,*" Markassie exclaimed, using the Inuktitut word for walrus. "Most important animal for Iglulik people. In the old days, if you didn't get any aiviq, you had to eat your aunt or uncle or someone like that ..."

We were now no more than than thirty feet from the floe, so I could see the walrus quite clearly. Alternately chummy and argumentative, they looked not unlike a group of venerable politicians holding a caucus, or perhaps a coterie of old military men reminiscing hoarsely about a long-forgotten campaign in some obscure corner of the globe.

And yet I also felt that I was witnessing a genuinely primordial spectacle, one that I could have witnessed just as readily during the last Ice Age, ten thousand or so years ago, as today. Indeed, I was so absorbed by this spectacle that I forgot to bring out my camera and take pictures of it.

When we got several feet closer, Markassie cut the motor. He didn't want to disturb the walrus, he said. For a disturbed walrus is an aggressive walrus. And an aggressive walrus might try to defend its territory by attacking the boat.

But these walrus were not aggressive at all. Quite the contrary. Once they became aware of our presence, they waddled off to the edge of the ice and dove into the sea. A while later their tusked heads surfaced as a group, bobbed for a minute or two, snuffled loudly, disappeared, and then surfaced again, regarding us with at best mild curiosity.

A single old bull stood his ground, however, and gave me a long hard stare with such excessively bloodshot eyes that I wondered if he'd been taking the odd tipple. I stared right back, for I happen to enjoy long staring sessions with animals. I believe they sense in me a kindred mental lethargy, a laziness, of sorts, that has them saying to themselves: "How similar to us is this peculiar human being."

And as I stared at this creature, this 3,000-pound fellow mammalian endowed with whiskers, flippers, and formidable tusks, I could not help but conclude that I was staring at something altogether outrageous, and altogether splendid.

Now we started home. On the way back, we stopped off at a small, uninhabited island called Qaigsuit thirty or so miles northeast of Iglulik. Long ago, this island had been occupied by the ancestors of today's Inuit, the so-called Thule people. According to Captain Parry's journal, they'd cut a path into Qaigsuit's rock merely by walking back and forth, back and forth, for centuries; and now I wanted to see if this path was still there, still insinuating itself into the island's geology.

I found the path without difficulty. Then I followed it around the island, past tent rings, kayak stands, and the huddled ruins of sod houses. Here and there I noticed a broken seal-oil lamp lying on the ground. And everywhere, in every cranny and crevice, I saw the vagrant bones of seals and walrus ... floating ribs, clavicles, scapulas, vertebrae, skulls, and whatever the plural of coccyx is. All these bones made me realize that I could have had exactly the same dining experience five hundred years ago on Qaigsuit as I'd had the day before in Iglulik.

And as I walked around this extraordinary boneyard, I heard no sound, none whatsoever, except the expostulating croaks of a raven. Once the raven flew away, however, the island's silence was so complete that it brought a slight whistling to my ears. At least I *think* it was the silence that did this, and not some belated Thule person whistling in astonishment at the presence of a visitor.

It was approaching midnight by the time we arrived back in Iglulik. But the sun was still out, bathing everything, from the most vocal sled dog to the lowliest chunk of early Paleozoic gravel, in a rich purple-grey light. This light was so bright that I could have read a newspaper by it if I so desired. But there are no newspapers in Iglulik. No bookstores, either. So instead of reading, I sat awake listening to the local dog population perform a little night-music.

And thus ends another day at the top of the world.

DINING OUT
WITH THE CREE

✻

There are certain parts of the world which would seem to be immune to automotive vehicles: Antarctica, the Amazon rainforest, the Himalayas, the Arabian Desert, and the taiga of northern Quebec. Then how come I was jolting along through the last-named of these geographies in a pickup truck?

I was helping my Cree friends David and Anna Bosum with a summer/fall ecotourism project that would give visitors a window on their traditional life in the bush. So I told them to take me into the bush and do unto me exactly what they'd do unto these prospective ecotourists.

I'd already gone on a winter/spring bush trip with David and Anna; a trip where we'd camped in the snowed-up woods a short distance from their village, Oujé-Bougoumou. But now they seemed to have taken the word bush literally, and we were venturing deep into heart of Canada's forest primeval.

The further we drove, the more primeval the road itself became, with a sand trap, a pothole, a boreal bog, a boulder, or a rippling stream every hundred feet. This made the pickup sway, vibrate, and sashay like an exotic dancer. And since I wasn't accustomed to being a passenger on an exotic dancer, I was starting to feel a little sick.

But I *was* sick, too. For two weeks I'd had a cold that seemed on the verge of bronchitis. And now, against my better judgment, I was heading off on an expedition seemingly calculated to make that bronchitis a living, gasping reality.

After four rough-and-tumble hours on the road, we arrived at our destination—a Cree campsite on the shore of Waposite Lake. We pitched our tents in a wind that threatened to blow them all the way down to Montreal, eight hundred miles due south of here. Later, when I went out in the middle of the night to answer Nature's proverbial call, I stepped right into the lake. Half asleep, I kept on walking until I realized that I was almost up to my knees in water.

Uh-oh, I told myself: now I'll probably come down with pneumonia.

It was raining when I woke up the next morning, although the temperature seemed cold enough for snow. Coughing and wheezing, I stumbled into David and Anna's tent, then plunked myself wearily down on its spruce bough floor. Kill me, I felt like telling them, and put an end to my misery. But they took one look at their ailing charge and plotted a course of action.

First, David went out and picked some Labrador tea. He boiled this heath shrub for half an hour, leaves, branches, and all, then poured the resulting brownish liquid into my cup.

"We call Labrador tea *katcibogotik,*" he told me. "That means 'the plant which does not die.' We pick it in winter, in the summer, all the time. You, too, won't die if you drink this tea. At least you won't die right now ..."

Comforting words! But I did in fact feel better after drinking a cup of the somewhat acrid-tasting tea. So I drank a second cup as well. And then a third.

"Don't worry, Larry," Anna smiled. "We have bush remedies for almost everything. So go ahead and get sick, it doesn't matter. You can even fall into the lake if you like."

Then she mentioned the following bush remedies:

Juice from the glands of a beaver, squirted in the eyes, will cure snowblindness. Frog piss heals insect bites. Eat the raw flesh of a mink if you're suffering from hypothermia. And if you suffer from heart trouble, put some bear piss in your tea—it'll make your ticker as good as new in practically no time.

More comforting words! Now I was worried not only about getting sick on this trip, but about getting well, too.

David handed me a moose's leg bone. If I gnawed at its sinews, he told me, I would get the strength back in my own legs. So I gnawed away. And although my legs did not feel any stronger, my teeth certainly did.

After I finished, David splintered the bone and removed a broken strip of marrow, which he dropped into a stewpot and then boiled into a thin grey broth. This was *mooskimee,* the Cree chicken soup. Skimming off some of the thick foam floating on the broth, he offered it to me. "Have some *mooskawanu,*" he said. It tasted not unlike ice cream ... if you can imagine a hot, viscous, moose-flavored ice cream.

As for the marrow broth itself, its taste was so strongly medicinal that it called up images of childhood illnesses and my mother spooning various indeterminate liquids to me.

By mid-afternoon, I felt well enough to go out with David on Waposite Lake. We paddled his canoe to a cove where he set down his fish net. On the way back, we paddled into the teeth of a robust wind that gave the canoe a robust life of its own. This wind also blew directly into my sinuses. By the time we reached the shore, I felt a relapse coming on.

No problem. No relapse, either. I just drank some more *katcibogotik* and *mooskimee.*

For supper, Anna cooked up a veritable smorgasbord of Cree traditional dishes: partridge liver boiled in the partridge's own crop;

rabbit dumplings; beaver tail; beaver cutlets garnished with bear grease; and bannock flavored with fish eggs.

After this hearty meal, I felt like I could go out and slay an *adoose* without suffering the consequences. In Cree mythology, an adoose is a cannibalistic giant similar to the better known *windigo*. The usual consequence of trying to do battle with one is mortal, followed by your immediate transformation into cuisine.

I didn't slay an adoose that night. Nor did I become a meal for one. For David and Anna had something else planned—a scapula divination. This ritual, known among the Cree as a *mitunsaawaakan*, dates back to the last Ice Age, when nomadic hunters all across the North used it to determine the whereabouts of game.

Affixing a rabbit's scapula bone to the end of a stick, David put it in the fire. He kept it there for a minute or so, warning me not to look at it. "It's very bad luck to look at a scapula while it's still in the fire," he told me.

"What would happen if I did look at it?" I said.

"You would die."

"How soon?"

"Maybe tomorrow, maybe next week."

It goes without saying that I didn't look at the scapula.

Now David took out the bone and proceeded to "read" its cracks and char marks.

"The rabbit sees a hill across the lake. There might be some game over there, maybe a moose or a caribou. The rabbit is trying to see this game, but he can't see anything for sure. There're too many clouds in the sky."

"Does the rabbit see any game closer to our campsite?" I asked him.

"There are too many clouds above us, too."

"And does the rabbit see anything that might relate to me? Like whether or not I'll come down with pneumonia as a result of this trip?"

"The rabbit doesn't know the answer to that question," David remarked. "But if you ask me, I think you'll be just fine ..."

By the time I got up the next morning, David had already paid a visit to his net. At the bottom of his canoe was a pile of whitefish, pickerel, and speckled trout ready to be smoked, dried, or cooked.

Now Anna made *shekaauwn,* a Cree specialty that combines fillets of fish, fish intestines, and blueberries, all cooked in bear grease. "Shekaauwn is a very healthy food," she said.

I put some in my mouth. It tasted not only healthy, but delicious, too. So delicious that I wouldn't have traded my plate of shekaauwn for all the truffles in Lyons.

And so it went for the better part of a week. Whenever I seemed to falter, my hosts would offer me some time-honored restorative from the Cree larder. By the end of the trip, I was feeling fine ... just as David had predicted.

Actually, I was feeling better than fine. On the jolting, rollicking, tooth-rattling drive back to Oujé-Bougoumou, I found myself dancing right along with the truck.

So if this story has any moral, it's this: The deeper you travel into the bush, the better the medicine.

ARCTIC DISCOVERY

In travel, as in life, context is everything. It's not likely that anyone would pay much attention to a traffic jam in Manhattan, whereas a traffic jam in Tiniteqilaq, East Greenland, would be a remarkable event, maybe even a disturbing one. For there are no roads in Tiniteqilaq. No cars, either.

I've never actually witnessed a traffic jam in the Arctic. But I have set foot on an arctic beach, Labrador's Porcupine Strand, which was as perfect as any beach featured on a travel poster ... except, of course, for its dead whales. And the best tan I've ever gotten did not come from the usual tanning zones in the Caribbean, the Greek isles, or the Pacific; it came from the Greenland Ice Cap.

Context, I've learned, has a way of making the ordinary seem extraordinary.

Last summer I found myself in the Arctic again—this time on Canada's Baffin Island. Accompanied by an Inuit guide, Peter Tunnillie, I was canoeing a segment of the Soper River on that island's remote Meta Incognita Peninsula.

River trips usually put me in mind of Huck Finn paddling the murky Mississippi or Thoreau enjoying a gentle meander on the Concord or Merrimack. But this one did not call up such comfortable literary associations. For the Soper is neither murky or gentle.

Nor does a single human being live along or even near its frigid 60-mile course.

River trips also call up images of vines, creepers, and lavish flora for me. But the country on either side of our canoe seemed nearly as bare as an old golf ball. It bore this bareness with rock-ribbed dignity, however. Greenery you can always get in the facile tropics, it seemed to say: I can offer you naked geology such as the earth itself possessed when its crust was first squeezed into shape.

As I silently regarded this geography, Peter said: "There's something really interesting I want to show you."

"What's that?" I asked him.

"Oh, I can't tell you now. It's a surprise. But you'll find out soon enough."

My mind raced through the possibilities: Perhaps Peter had discovered the skeletal remains of Martin Frobisher's so-called "Five Missing Men"—five crewmen who disappeared on this peninsula while serving on an expedition with Frobisher, a sixteenth-century arctic explorer. Or maybe there was a group of uncontacted Inuit somewhere in the vicinity. Or maybe a significant archaeological site ...

But he merely shook his head, smiling mysteriously, in response to my questions. After all, this was supposed to be a surprise.

When we put ashore for lunch, I gave Peter some dried whale meat I'd gotten a week earlier in Iglulik; he gave me some of his noodle soup. *Qallunaaq* (white man) and Inuk, we seemed to be moving inexorably toward the other's diet.

Later we walked inland a short distance. I gathered some small, reddish mushrooms which, according to Peter, the local lemmings use as an aphrodisiac. Then we visited a lapis lazuli mine that'd been abandoned many years ago. Scattered over the ground was a veritable mosaic of dusky blue lapis gemstones.

I asked Peter if this unexpected beauty was in fact his surprise. He shook his head again. It wasn't.

Now we returned to the canoe. Shortly after we moved on, I began to notice caribou by the hundreds browsing the mossy banks along the river. They would lift their heads and stare at us with utter bewilderment, as if they'd never encountered non-antlered beings before.

This wasn't the surprise, either. For Peter knew that I, as an old arctic hand, had seen plenty of caribou in my day.

Immediately after we negotiated a series of loops in the river, Peter pointed to a lofty escarpment in the distance. "See the rock that looks like a woman with a baby in her *amauti?*" he said. "Just below it is where we're going."

Putting ashore again, we began to hike toward this woman-shaped rock. The suspense, I admit, was killing me. I tried to re-member if any of Sir John Franklin's ill-fated crew had ended up on Baffin Island ... or if I'd read about an endangered species which nested, denned, or burrowed in these parts.

We hiked into a valley where the vegetation seemed altogether luxuriant compared to before. I saw the gossamer tufts of arctic cotton, Lapland rosebay, harebells, saxifrages, moss campion, and several different types of berries. Meanwhile, hordes of mosquitoes were mobbing my every pore, even probing the eyelets of my boots.

At last we arrived at a clump of arctic willows not quite ten feet high.

"There!" Peter exclaimed triumphantly. "The only trees on Baffin Island!"

Over the years I had seen plenty of trees, of course. But to find trees in such hard country—even stunted, minimal trees like these—seemed to me almost unimaginable. In fact, I was as surprised by this wisp of a forest as I would have been by a herd of caribou on Boston Common.

"Photo?" Peter asked. I nodded and handed him my camera.

And now, over a year later, the picture he took occupies pride of place on the bulletin board above my desk. It shows me standing in front of a tangle of branches that look not unlike chickenwire. On my face is an expression of distinct astonishment.

How, friends ask me, can you be astonished by such a seemingly ordinary scene?

Context is everything, I tell them.

THE CALL OF
THE YUKON

A turn-of-the-century photograph shows a ragtag trio of men recently arrived in Dawson City, boom town of the Klondike gold rush. Having braved half a continent, climbed the icy Chilkoot Pass, and poled a skiff five hundred miles down the Yukon River, they've just now found out the cruel truth: virtually all the mining claims around Dawson have been staked. Yet the men's faces don't show despair, nor even disappointment, but something akin to exhilaration. It's as if the promise of gold were simply an excuse to take in the unsullied air of the Yukon for a while.

Canada's Yukon Territory has always been more than a mere geographical setting. It has the quality of an ideal, or an experience, or perhaps a summons to march to a distinctly different drummer. It attracts in nearly equal numbers gold miners, homesteaders, and refugees from law and order. And yet it remains itself, wholly eccentric. Where else can you find world-class outhouse races, individually heated parking meters, and enormous cast-iron mosquitoes used as lawn ornaments? Atop a mountain near Keno City there's a signpost indicating the distance to, among other places, Tahiti. Keno City itself has a house built almost entirely of beer bottles, 32,000 of them, in fact. According to the owner, they help insulate the house against winters that otherwise would freeze his hair to his pillow.

Summers, I ought to add, are a bit less severe. It's not unusual for either Dawson or the territorial capital of Whitehorse to be the warmest spot in Canada a couple of times each summer. One July day in Dawson I walked uphill into the steaming bush, toward the so-called Moosehide Slide, and I nearly could have imagined myself in a tropical rainforest, so thick and florid was the vegetation, so earthy its scent. But I was only a hundred miles below the Arctic Circle. So much for the cliché about such latitudes being ruthlessly desolate.

The Yukon is likely to catch even the inveterate northern traveler by surprise. Consider the Gwichin Indian village of Old Crow. I'd expected it to be a place afloat with rubbish, animal bones, disembowelled mattresses, and cast-off snowmobile parts—typical northern landscaping. Instead I found a tidy little town, all neatness and order, with nary a discarded candy wrapper in sight. I didn't see any food scraps, either. Old Crow's myriad ravens, perched on rooftops or waddling brazenly down the middle of the road, saw to that. Indeed, the town derives its name from these gluttonous ravens, called crows by the Gwichin.

In Old Crow, I paid a visit to Edith Josey, the local correspondent for the *Whitehorse Star* and a legend in her own time. For thirty years Miss Josey has been regaling her readers with weather reports, births, funerals, and the minutiae of muskrat trapping. She writes her columns exactly the way she speaks. "Here are the news" [sic] she'll announce at the beginning of a column, then go on to comment on the local scene with observations like "Sure lots of fish this year" and "Old Crow sure quite lonesome town, but sure nice little town." Yukoners, tolerating—nay, celebrating—idiosyncracy, praise Miss Josey for the strength and purity of her prose style.

Old Crow *is* a nice little town. In 1941, Gwichin Chief Peter Moses heard about the German bombing of London over his wireless. Hundreds of children, the news report said, were homeless. The Chief raised seven hundred dollars from his sympathetic constituents in Old Crow, mostly through the sale of muskrat pelts, and sent the money to the children of bomb-ravaged London. A highly altruistic gesture from one group of have-nots to another.

But I did not find Dawson a very nice town. More precisely, I found it rather too nice. Gone, long gone was the brawling, lusty, cheerfully irreverent boom town in which lived such worthies as Jack London, Arizona Charlie Meadows, and Nelly the Pig, the last so named because she once bit off an abusive miner's ear. In its place was Gold Rush kitsch, an entire town tarted up Gay Nineties style for the sake of tourists. Streets were lined with immaculate false-front buildings, some painted yellow, a couple horrendously pink, most purveying latter-day Klondike trinkets. Not one showed its true age except perhaps the old gun and ammunition depot, a jumble—a quite attractive jumble, I dare say—of crumbling boards.

One afternoon I visited the log cabin where Robert Service, Bard of the Yukon and ex-President Reagan's favorite poet, once lived. No less than a hundred other visitors had the same idea, for there they sat in front of Service's cabin, row upon row of them, listening to a man in period costume recite from the poet's high-flown doggerel.

"The wild is calling, calling ... let us go!" incanted the man.

And so I went ... to Diamond Tooth Gertie's. During the gold rush, Gertie's was a celebrated den of iniquity, a place where you could get a drink, a woman, or a fist in the jaw, often at the same time. In its present incarnation, I found it hardly more naughty than a church bazaar. But then I don't tend to find can-can dancing or roulette croupiers in period costume especially naughty.

Inside Gertie's I approached a barman in a bowler hat, gartered sleeves, and a handlebar mustache. Putting on my best vengeful miner's voice, I growled: "I'm looking for a woman named Nelly the Pig."

"I'm sorry, sir," the barman said politely, "but I don't recognize the name. Does she live in Dawson?"

I shook my head sadly. *Sic transit gloria mundi!*

But Dawson does possess at least one extraordinary sight: itself. Much of the town lists, now to the starboard, now to port, as a result of the permafrost's incessant thawing and freezing action. My hotel was humpbacked, the mortuary was swaybacked, and Madame Tremblay's Store was both. In certain buildings the permafrost had given windows peculiar squints or suspended them in midyawn. The board sidewalks achieved such meandering contours that they might have been laid out by a team of terminally drunk carpenters.

Aha, I thought to myself, Nature triumphs over Disneyland. I was so cheered by this triumph that I walked right into the Sluicebox Bar and plunked down twelve dollars for the *specialité de la maison*— a Sourtoe Cocktail, named for the toe, reputedly frostbitten, then amputated, then pickled, which gives the drink its inimitable flavor. On at least one occasion, the toe has been accidentally swallowed. No problem: the Yukon abounds with frostbitten toes, and it could be easily replaced.

I was cheered by the same phenomenon in every corner of the Yukon. Man's works always seemed to be atilt, askew, or somehow awry, the playthings of a whimsical Nature. As for Man himself, he too was a plaything, his tenure brief, his legacy usually a rotting cabin invaded by lupines and wild roses. Just look at these statistics: Dawson, which once boasted a population of 35,000, now has fewer than 1,500 people; Keno City had 20,000 people during the 1920s silver boom, but now has no more than twenty people; Keno City's neighbor, Elsa, once a community of 1,200, has only four stalwart citizens; and Herschel Island, which had almost 2,000 whalers, Inuit, and missionaries at the turn of the century, doesn't have a single year-round inhabitant today.

As a wag in Keno City said to me, the Yukon is a place with lots of space, most of it empty. Although twice the size of New England, nowadays it has fewer people than Portsmouth, New Hampshire. One can tramp around for days, maybe even weeks, and not see a single soul. Not a single human soul, that is.

One evening in Kluane (pronounced Kloo-*wan*-ee) Park, I counted forty-three Dall sheep rams headbutting each other on the mountain above my campsite; a mountain named, appropriately enough, Sheep Mountain. The next day I saw half a dozen eagles in various stages of predation. One eagle was hovering in desultory fashion over a lake when suddenly it dropped down to grab a jackfish. The fish dove into the depths of the lake with the eagle still clinging to it. When it surfaced again, the drowned eagle lay across its back like a crumpled dish rag.

There is one creature who's a partner, sometimes invisible, sometimes not, on every Kluane jaunt. I refer to *Ursus horribilis,* otherwise known as grizzly bear. Kluane has the highest concentration of grizzlies in Canada. And the Slims River area has the highest concentration of them in Kluane. A fact which turned every bush into a bear when I went hiking there.

"Just make a racket so griz'll know we're coming," my guide said, and proceeded to bang away at the frame of his backpack with a cup. To the casual listener, he must have sounded a bit like an unhealthy radiator. I must have sounded like an escaped madman myself, for I was singing "The Teddy Bear's Picnic" over and over again, the better to warn any lurking grizzlies of our peaceful intentions. Whether this unholy clamor worked I don't know, but we didn't encounter any bears on the trip. Plenty of scat and prints, but not griz himself. This left me feeling both relieved and disappointed. On the one hand, I was delighted not to have met an animal capable of sending me to my Maker with a more or less casual flip of its paw. On the other hand, I'd hoped to see (from a distance, of course) one of these grandiose mountains of fur and ferocity, now considerably endangered elsewhere in North America.

In fact, I did see a grizzly a week or so later. It happened when I least expected it, as my plane banked just prior to landing on Herschel Island. Bears are not native to Herschel, so this particular animal—a small brown patch fleeing the Cessna's monstrous shadow—must have wandered over from the mainland the previous winter, when the Beaufort Sea formed an ice bridge, and now was stranded here.

"There goes Mr. Son of a Bitch!" declared the pilot admiringly as the bear disappeared behind a tussocky rise. That was all I saw of it—one momentary, privileged glimpse. And then the plane touched down on Herschel.

From 1894 to 1905, this small island at the northern tip of the Yukon was the headquarters for whaling in the Arctic. It was, depending on whose account you wish to believe, either "an outpost of civilization" (explorer Vilhjalmur Stefansson) or "the Sodom and Gomorrah of the Ice-Fields" (Alaska newspaper, 1905). Today, however, it is a place where the visitor sees only the ghosts of time: rusting metal, derelict buildings, boats left high and dry, and coffins pushed up brokenly by the permafrost. From the ice-floes come tendrils of mist, the island's winding-sheet, and off in the empty distances foxes bark a shrill requiem. Herschel is what Dawson isn't; a place that has died with dignity.

A melancholy place? Not at all. Or at least not during the short arctic summer, when round-the-clock photosynthesis gives the island a carpet of infinitely delicate wildflowers, beluga and bowhead whales frolic just offshore, Pauline Cove is full of moulting seabirds, and black guillemots nest in the old Anglican church.

Then Herschel, although remote in sensation, will seem not unlike certain ruggedly handsome, bird-rich, people-poor islands in the west of Ireland or the Scottish Hebrides.

Except there's the difference of the sun. No Irish or Hebridean sun, assuming one exists, is quite like the Herschel sun. It shines at midday, midnight, and three o'clock in the morning. It shines even when it's setting and then, a giant refreshed, it seems to shine all the more brilliantly. On permafrost, tussocks, graves, old blubber houses, the Northern Whaling and Trading Company Store, and the aviary-church, it shines. And so magical is its high latitude light that one can perhaps be forgiven for thinking this lump of frozen Yukon mud heaven on earth.

ONE MAN'S MIRACLE

I am by inclination a devotee of quirky churches. There's the church in the Inuit village of Inuvik that's shaped like a sort of extraterrestrial igloo. Then there's the church in New Ipswich, New Hampshire, which doubles as a pizza parlor.

Then, of course, there's the tiny Mödrudalur church in Iceland. It is a building I wouldn't trade for Westminster Abbey, Chartres, or the Cologne Cathedral, not even if you threw in their crypts, too. Why I'm so fond of it you'll learn shortly, but first let me describe Mödrudalur and the man who made this farm, one of Iceland's most isolated, his hearth for more than forty years.

Mödrudalur lies under the icy nipple of Mt. Herdubreid in the northeast corner of the island. All around it is a broad highland plateau whose sintery ground is a pale dun color barely relieved by clumps of grass. Wind devils whip up swirls of sand and blow them along until they spank against volcanic ash heaps. At any moment, you expect to see a group of Bedouins emerge from a sandstorm or hear a muezzin's nasal *Lā ilāh illā Allāh.*

Like most Icelandic farms, Mödrudalur has a resident ghost. This ghost, Margaret, mostly keeps to the kitchen and knits socks, but every once in a while she'll venture out and kill a few sheep as revenge against her philandering, sheep-farming husband, dead these several hundred years. At least that's the explanation usually given for why sheep seem to die here so unexpectedly.

But there's more to Mödrudalur than sand and ghosts. The best *hangikjöt* (wind-cured lamb) in Iceland reputedly comes from here. If only for that reason, the farm never seems to lack prospective buyers.

In 1919, a man named Jón Stefánsson bought Mödrudalur from his brothers. Jón was a saddler and harness maker by trade. A recipe of his for curing leather with sheep brains and rancid butter is still extant in certain parts of the island. The farm's curious terrain seems to have inspired him. There's nothing for miles around but derelict space and the effects of a free-wheeling geology. At night he'd sit at his organ and the echo of Bach toccatas, which he'd play backwards note for note, would sweep over Mödrudalur's empty sands and scoria craters.

Jón was, to put it mildly, an eccentric. He'd wake up at four in the morning and get the farm laborers working furiously on some outlandish project. Then he'd forget the purpose of this project and wander off by himself, playing his fiddle. Playing it, that is, until noon. At noon he'd stop and sneeze. If you want to live to a ripe old age, he'd say, you must sneeze punctually at noon. (Jón himself lived to well over ninety.)

There'd been a church at Mödrudalur in saga times. But when Jón purchased the farm, this church was in a hopeless state of disrepair. Jón used the pulpit for storing saltfish and probably would have wintered his sheep in the nave were it not for the absence of a roof.

In 1949, Jón's wife died. He decided to build a new church as a memorial to her. He didn't have a plan for this church, so he sat down, drank a few cups of strong coffee, and drew up a plan in six minutes. He built it in a little less than two years. He wanted to carve his wife's name above the threshhold, but the local Bishop said he wouldn't consecrate a house of God that was dedicated to a mere human being rather than a religious figure. Jón protested that his wife *was* a religious figure. At least more so than some forgotten Italian virgin of the tenth century. In the end, however, he had to settle for an altarpiece of his own creation.

Not long ago, on an Iceland trip, I visited Mödrudalur myself. The old churchyard was raised up from the meager ground like an Irish potato bed. Here I found the graves of Jón Stefánsson and his wife. Nearby was the grave of the ghost Margaret ... a considerably less satisfactory lodging than a farmhouse's cozy kitchen.

Here, too, was Jón's church. It was in the standard designer style of Icelandic country churches—white, rectangular, steepleless, unassuming. But even for an Icelandic country church, it was quite small. Doubtless an elderly man would not have wanted to embark on a full-scale cathedral, but this edifice, if I may call it that, was hardly the size of a single-car garage. It had room for maybe ten steadfast parishioners. Anyone else would have to stand outside and commune with his Maker via the infinitely various Icelandic elements.

Above the pulpit was Jón's altarpiece, which depicts Mt. Herdubreid. On the mountain's usually wind-blasted and snow-encased summit Jón had painted an orchard of palm trees. He'd also established a base camp of Giotto-style supplicants at the foot of the mountain. The main figure was Christ Himself, who was sliding down Herdubreid's vertiginous slopes with arms outstretched.

Jón hadn't bothered to give any of the supplicants faces. Christ was more fortunate and possessed a face. But Jón didn't draw it. His half-brother Haukur did. "Haukur's better at faces than I am," Jón reportedly said. (Haukur was a house-painter in Akureyri at the time.)

The more I gazed at the painting, the more endangered Christ's position looked to me. I wondered whether He was going to end up in a heap at the bottom of Herdubreid, a mountaineering casualty. Then I recalled what Jón had told someone who'd voiced a similar concern: "No, He won't fall down the mountain. You can't see them, but I painted holes in the rock for His heels ..."

I confess I left Jón Stefánsson's church—a building you won't find in any tourist guide or historical register—in an attitude of, if not quite exaltation, at least exalted good cheer. It was a monument to the human spirit. Even more, it was a monument to human whimsy. And somehow it seemed perfectly appropriate for a place that, on the verge of the Arctic Circle, blows sandstorms.

LAWRENCE MILLMAN

TRAVELS IN
THE BARREN LANDS

Seldom if ever had I encountered a more exotic cause of stomach upset than the one I heard about from the copper-faced, significantly withered old man, who told me: "I have a dog in my gut that's bothering me. When I was young, I had a pretty good dog team. But one of my dogs wasn't working too well, so I killed him. My father said, 'That dog will come back and get revenge on you for what you did to him.' Well, my father was right. The dog is here, right here, in my stomach."

Where can the jaded traveler hear admissions like this? In Keewatin, of course.

Keewatin, which means "north wind" in native parlance, is the district in Canada's Northwest Territories west of Hudson Bay, bordered on the south by the 60th parallel and on the north by the Arctic Circle. Although roughly the same size as France, it has fewer than five thousand people, most of whom are—like my canine-dyspeptic old man—Inuit.

That equation of people to land area ranks Keewatin with Siberia and the Australian outback in the Emptiness Sweepstakes. Step a few feet outside any of its seven small communities and you'll find yourself in unpeopled tundra, a landscape of jewel-like lakes, glacial excoriations, rock sculptures, and lichen tapestries. Presiding over this landscape is a vast, apparently horizonless sky; a sky capable of exploding into a purple and orange sunset that makes one of J.M.W. Turner's painted sunsets seem like a shabby affair indeed.

Be forewarned, however. Keewatin will not overwhelm you with its touristic amenities or fifth-arrondissement comforts. Rather than fleshpots, it'll offer you what might be called bone-pots—the skeletal remains of animals seemingly preserved forever on the tundra. Even the capital, Rankin Inlet, has no obvious sights to see unless you consider a defunct nickel mine a sight. Nor is there a single pub, boutique, newsstand, tobacconist, or Chinese restaurant in the entire district. Rankin Inlet does have a yacht club, but no yachts. The club throws an annual dinner complete with monogrammed cutlery to enliven the year-round non-yachting season.

Keewatin's attractions are subtle, often fleeting, a host of shifting colors and inexplicable moments. I experienced one such moment when I raised my camera to photograph some caribou grazing on a ridge near Repulse Bay. My Inuit guide stuck his hand in front of my lens.

"No picture," he said.

"Why not?" I asked.

"Spirit Caribou," was his answer. And when I looked back, the caribou had in fact disappeared. Whether they had entered a spiritual realm or were merely grazing on the other side of the ridge, I'll never know.

And then there was the case of the missing bones. This happened at Ferguson Lake, a lake which boasts twenty-five-pound trout (twenty-five-pound mosquitoes, I'm convinced, too). I'd gone there not for the fishing, but simply to hang out at a place a hundred and fifty miles from the nearest telephone. One day I visited the mound of stones known locally as "the shaman's grave." Only the previous week, I'd been told, a grinning skull, some rib ends, and a pair of femurs had been plainly visible through the chinks and holes. But now, when I peered in, I could discern no shamanic bones whatsoever. Then I noticed a very large musk ox staring rather intently at me. Since Inuit shamans in death as in life can take on animal form, I decided to beat out a hasty retreat ... and go fishing.

Amid such strange appearances and disappearances, it is Keewatin's stones themselves that endure. Beside rivers and lakes you'll see ring after ring of them, mute testimony to a time when the Inuit, instead of living in prefab houses, lived in caribou-hide tents. Along the Meliadine River I visited a five-hundred-year-old archaeological site that was a teeming metropolis of stone, with tent rings, meat caches, kayak stands, graves, and boulders used for hopping contests. I could easily imagine the Meliadine people going about their daily lives here—some men setting up a fish weir, teenagers hopping blithely over the boulders, maybe an elder telling an old story or two to his grandchildren.

Such was the idyllic existence of the so-called Caribou Inuit. Except that it often led to a quite unidyllic phenomenon, starvation, when the caribou didn't show up. Imagine the prospect of your own clothing as cuisine and you'll appreciate at least one Inuit winter pastime. It was a pastime that continued until the late 1950s, when the last nomadic Inuit exchanged their bush camps for a more or less settled life in Baker Lake. Rather than rely on the whims of caribou, they could stroll over to the Hudson Bay trading post and stock up on tinned peas. Tinned peas do not migrate. Or fail to migrate.

Baker Lake, Canada's only inland Inuit community, is a motley collection of jerrybuilt houses deposited alongside a formidable lake of the same name. You'd think that one blast from a strong wind would blow the whole town into the lake. Yet despite (or perhaps because of) its seeming impermanence, Baker Lake is Keewatin's most appealing town. Local women still carry their babies in *amaut* sacks on their backs, and drying caribou skins hang next to drying laundry on clotheslines. So abundant are diminutive all-terrain vehicles (ATVs) that they give the town a cheerfully Lilliputian, almost cartoonish quality.

Remote it might be, but Baker Lake is no cultural backwater. Quite the contrary. You can't throw a rock over one of its ATVs without hitting an artist. Here sits a man with his chisel, slowly, laboriously transforming the sweeping curves of a musk ox horn into a long-necked goose. His next door neighbor is carving a block of black soapstone into an heroic whale. Indeed, half the town's adults have sold a print, tapestry, or carving to a gallery down south, something which doubtless would make Montparnasse green with envy.

Whence comes this creative ferment? Possibly, it's a survival from the days when a person was obliged to fashion all his tools, clothing, and objects of amusement himself. It could also come from possessing an especially observant pair of eyes. For example: One carver I met was working an old piece of whalebone. In the bone's pitted textures I watched a bear, albeit a bear with flippers and antlers, take shape. Declared the carver: "You haven't seen one of these creatures before? I see them all the time..."

Later this same carver took a piece of string and showed me a string picture of a man being chased by, and then eaten by, a polar bear. Then he showed me two arctic hares enjoying each other carnally. It struck me that this ancient art form, called *ayayaq* by the Inuit, is probably the earliest type of motion picture ever conceived.

Not far from Baker Lake, at the mouth of the Thelon River, is a traditional camp set up to provide visitors with a window on the Inuit past. I don't care for calculated traditionality (natives shedding their jeans for loincloths and so on), so I wasn't too eager to visit this camp. I went there only at the insistence of my Inuit hosts.

But I still wasn't too happy about it. To be genuinely traditional, I told the boatman, these camp dwellers will have to be at the end of their respective tethers, starving, in fact.

How wrong I was about the camp. It turned out not to be a "window" on the past, solemnly educational, but the past itself. In residence was an elderly couple who were a mere generation away from living off the land. They exhibited the tools of their subsistence, including a caribou scapula specifically designed to remove fecal matter from one's tent. Both the man and woman had been born heathens, a fact I found curiously gratifying. The man told me that he was quite unimpressed when he first heard about Christ walking on water. Didn't his own people walk on water all the time —in winter? Then he gestured to his stomach and mentioned a certain dog that'd been bothering him ...

Rather than return to Baker Lake by boat, I took the overland route. From the camp I ascended a low ridge, then began walking along a broad undulating plain. Every once in a while an arctic ground squirrel would cite me for trespass by squeaking its Inuit name *siksik* repeatedly. A piebald cock ptarmigan drummed at me. And as I walked by, a pair of sandhill cranes took to the air with a series of surprised chortles.

In the absence of a trail, *inukshuks* marked the correct route to Baker Lake. These piles of rock, shaped like human sentinels, are the tundra's directional indicators. Wherever you go in Keewatin, you'll see them silhouetted eerily against the sky. Nothing else interrupts the smooth contours of the land except the fretwork of an occasional radio tower. Certainly there aren't any trees, any *real* trees, only eighteen-inch dwarf willows anchored to the shallow soil by their virtually naked roots.

This general treelessness is, I suspect, what provoked the eighteenth-century explorer Samuel Hearne to call Keewatin's topography "the Barren Lands." An inspired phrase, one that is still in use today, but a phrase hardly fair to the three hundred wildflower varieties, from Lapland rosebays to coral-root orchids, that bloom here each year. Nor is it fair to the hundred species of birds which seem to prefer nesting in Keewatin to nesting in a tree-blessed habitat. Nor is it quite fair to the cloudberries on which I happily dined a few miles into my tundra walk. No stout oak or stately elm could have equalled the succulent flavor of these berries.

Clearly, some redefinitions are in order. Maybe the word "barren" could henceforth be used to extol a certain type of austere beauty, as in "On my way to Baker Lake I passed through some splendidly barren country."

Most splendidly barren of all is Marble Island, a chunk of creamy-white quartzite thirty-five miles east of Rankin Inlet. According to legend, it was once an iceberg. An old Inuit lady, left there to die after the fashion of her people, prayed that she at least be allowed to die on solid ground. Her prayers were answered: the iceberg was transformed.

From a distance the island still looks a little like its previous incarnation. It also looks like some sort of white leviathan, Moby Dick perhaps, risen from the dull grey waters of Hudson Bay. Closer up, its slabs of upright, frost-hewn rock suggest a graveyard of giants. It would be a nuisance to crawl over them. Upon arrival, however, the visitor to Marble Island must get down on his hands and knees and literally crawl over a number of smaller, less sharp rocks. For only a submissive crawl will placate the old Inuit lady, the island's tutelary spirit. Anyone who walks, jogs, or hops ashore will die within a year and a day. Or so the story goes.

I'm a sucker for superstition, so I crawled ashore. My guide, a floridly-whiskered Rankin Inlet man named Bill Gawor, crawled ashore, too. So did Bill's son Feliks. Then we proceeded to put up our tents in a wind-protected hollow not far from James Knight's house site.

James Knight, presumably, did *not* crawl ashore. With his two ships, the *Albany* and the *Discovery*, he left England in June 1719 to search for the Northwest Passage. Having reached Hudson Bay, he decided to overwinter on Marble Island. And neither he or his forty men were ever seen or heard from again. Nor have their remains been found—artifacts like clay pipes and leather boots, yes, but no actual remains. What became of Knight and his men is a mystery that makes the better known mystery of the Franklin expedition seem like a Sunday-school picnic.

It's tempting to play amateur sleuth on Marble Island. Yet this unadorned geology hoards its secrets carefully. All we found from the Knight expedition was part of an oaken stanchion, probably from the *Albany*, with old-fashioned square nails hammered into it. On the other hand, there were plenty of tent rings and meat caches, evidence of a much earlier Inuit occupation. Inside the meat caches, grease from long ago had seeped into the ground and nourished it: the resulting lupines and chickweed would have passed for a botanical cornucopia elsewhere on the island.

Bill cautioned me to be on the alert for polar bears, whose white fur blends in perfectly with the island's own whiteness. Alert I was, but I didn't see any bears. I did see a peregrine falcon—a bird far more predacious than the average bear—swoop down on an unsuspecting golden plover, then carry it off to its cliffside lair. I also saw a spectacular display of northern lights, not anything to be particularly cautious about ... except in Keewatin. If you whistle at the northern lights, say the Inuit, they'll come down from the sky and smite you.

At one point I happened to lose a glove.

"The Old Lady's got it," Bill remarked, as if her repertoire included theft, along with snatching people into oblivion.

I found the glove a day later, which goes to show that the Old Lady might taketh away, but she likewise giveth. Gloves, exhilarating winds, thousand year-old lichens—those were just some of her gifts. Yet her most valuable gift of all was Marble Island itself, a barren, haunting, perhaps even haunted outpost of the North.

LAWRENCE MILLMAN

TAAKKUA UKALIUP
ANANGIT!

✤

Let's say that you'd like to travel somewhere different this year, some-where completely off the well-beaten, souvenir-littered touristic path. Antarctica is too expensive, Europe too cozy, and Afghani-stan not quite cozy enough. So, in spite of the fact that your travel agent doesn't have any brochures advertising it, or perhaps because of that fact, you decide to visit Labrador.

You fly from Goose Bay to Nain, then plunk your kayak in the cold Labrador Sea and begin paddling north along the hardbitten, granitic coastline. After a couple of days, you need to replenish your water supply, so you paddle over to an island with a small Inuit encampment on it.

As you're stepping ashore, a snaggle-toothed Inuk comes up to you and says in an urgent voice:

"Aunaagaalunganut tutiniannak!"

The man is speaking a guttural Eskimoan language, Inuttut, which you can't begin to understand. He may be telling you that tourism is punishable by death in these parts, or that the island has come down with the plague. Or perhaps he's just desperate for a cigarette. What do you do?

You reach for your *Labrador Inuit Uqausingit,* of course.

This dictionary-phrasebook, published in 1976 by the Labrador Inuit Committee on Literacy, will take you by the hand and walk you through virtually any situation you're likely to encounter in Inuttut. Not only that, but it'll also walk you through a number of situations you'll never encounter. For example, it'll tell you how to inform authorities that you're being stalked by a mountain lion ... even though there aren't any mountain lions in Labrador.

So let's get back to that snaggle-toothed Inuk. A quick check of your *uqausingit* will tell you exactly what he's saying. There is no plague on the island. Nor is he asking you for a cigarette. Rather, he's warning you not to step on that recently-flensed seal directly in front of you.

As you move briskly aside, he scoops up something brown and jellylike from the seal carcass and smilingly offers it to you. *"Puiji qagutanginnik nigilautsiin?"* he asks. (Would you care to eat some seal brains?)

You prefer *nunivaakka* (berries), you tell him. Like those succulent-looking ones you see only a few feet away. But just as you're reaching down to gather some, your friend grabs your arm. *"Taakkua ukaliup anangit,"* he exclaims. (Don't eat that. It's rabbit shit.)

Saved from a fate even worse than seal brains. But you are in fact rather hungry, so you ask him if there's any *pitsik* (dried fish) on the island.

He shakes his head. *"Tulugaaluit pitsinnik nigilittut."* (The damn crows have eaten all our dried fish.)

Before you can ask if there's any *nikku* (dried caribou meat), a small girl runs past you, screaming loudly, and hides behind a glacial erratic. "What's the matter with her?" you ask the man.

"Pillitammik qinajuk," he replies. (She is frightened of grasshoppers.)

"There's a little boy hiding behind that erratic, too."

"Paqaittausimakqajuk anagiattusimatauni." (He is embarrassed

because someone opened the outhouse door on him.)

"Some archaeologists are there, too."

"Saunikuvomaalummik naffaasimajuk." (They are looking for old skeletons.)

Now you ask about the *nikku*. Alas, the man says, the *tuttu* (caribou) have yet to make their appearance this year.

But he does invite you to his tent for supper. There you join his family for a meal of local specialties—*sungarnit* (ptarmigan intestines), *sikquk* (seal flipper), chunks of *utsuk* (blubber), and *aivik ammuumajuit* (the half-digested contents of a walrus' stomach). The last-named of these items looks like *luumikiik* (lube oil). Smearing a little on a piece of bannock, you learn that it tastes like luumikiik, too.

As you're eating, you listen to bits of conversation:

"Aikqavaugaakka milami qimanniqakkit." (I left my mittens outside, and the dogs ate them.)

"Uumajualuttaungituaguvit." (I hope a sea monster doesn't attack you.)

"Ajuqittuijuk ullumi qanimajuk." (The minister is very sick today. Perhaps he'll croak.)

"Itiqa ungilajuk." (My ass is itchy.)

Suddenly an old man rushes into the tent and exclaims:

"Uumaat? Noah umiatsuavininga naffaatausimalittuk!"

Is this fellow saying what you think he's saying? Right away you consult your uqausingit. There it is, the old man's very utterance, translated as follows on page 164:

Guess what? The ruins of Noah's ark have been found!

A jumble of questions floods your mind. Any sign of Noah himself? How intact was the ark? Was it discovered on Mount Ararat? in Asia Minor? or perhaps somewhere in Labrador?

But the man has already left. Since you want to find out more, you rise to follow him, but your host gestures for you to sit down.

The old man is an *angakkuk* (shaman), he tells you, and has already transformed himself into a *tingijuugaaluk* (jet plane) in order to convey this astonishing news to other Inuit encampments up and down the coast.

It's time for you to leave, too. For you have miles to paddle before you rest. So you shake hands all around and, fetching your water, head down to your kayak. Now your host smiles and bids you farewell:

"Aullasimaliguvit, ajutsajuujaalaalikquqot." (When you have gone, it will seem like we are very poor.)

Whereupon you begin paddling north again, ever grateful that you've brought along a good dictionary-phrasebook.

A VOYAGE AROUND
GWAII HAANAS

❋

On a typically glowering, drizzly day in British Columbia's Queen Charlotte Islands, I asked a Haida Indian elder named Nathan Young to call up his memories of fifty years ago and more. Soon he began telling me a story about his uncle. The old man would stand on the deck of his fishing boat as it entered some cove or inlet in the southern part of these islands. Then he would gaze toward land and shake his head almost in disbelief, saying over and over again:

"Gwaii Haanas! Gwaii Haanas!"

Although Nathan Young's uncle did not participate in the naming process, Gwaii Haanas also happens to be the name of the national park reserve that occupies the southern 15 percent of this far-flung archipelago. The words mean "Awesome Place," "Place of Wonder," or "Beautiful Islands," depending on which Haida does the translating.

Yet whatever the exact meaning, one thing is clear: those two words capture the essence of a realm that's like a cross between the legendary Horn of Plenty and Alice's Wonderland. It's a realm where Peale's peregrine falcons whistle through the air at speeds upwards of 200 mph; where bald eagles build nests that can be six feet across and weigh nearly two tons; where black bears grow so fat during salmon season that their bellies drag along the ground; where those same bears, lifting up rocks in search of crustaceans, gently replace them, as if unwilling to disturb the ecosystem; where cyanide bugs smell of almonds, and sea lions, if you get close enough to them, give off a smell of ineffable rankness; where brown bull kelp can grow as much as a foot in a single day; and where, thirty feet above the ground, the monstrous grin of a grizzly bear adorns a Haida mortuary pole.

Early in my trip, on the day my boat the *Kingii* put in at Windy Bay on Lyell Island, I received a strong foretaste of Gwaii Haanas' wonder-making ability myself. It was a day even more stubbornly unwondrous than the day I visited Nathan Young. A cold rain was slashing away at sea and shore, mountains and forest. Likewise a fog had crept in. Crept in not "on little cat's feet," as fogs often creep in poetry, but on the robust paws of a lion or tiger.

Rain and fog—the meteorological two-step of the Northwest. The former exalts flora to biblical dimensions and also swells up rivers so that salmon can swim upstream and spawn. As for the latter, it can draw a curtain of invisibility over whatever the former exalts. It was due largely to this curtain that European mariners did not approach the Queen Charlottes until the Spanish corvette *Santiago* dropped anchor here in 1774.

But however time-honored the weather, I was determined not to let it spoil my encounter with a place Haida sculptor Bill Reid once compared to the Peaceable Kingdom. So I donned my anorak, pocketed my compass, and went ashore. Soon I found myself walking through, if not the Peaceable Kingdom, at least a boreal variation on the theme of Amazonian lushness. Sitka spruce and western red cedars soared Biblically two hundred feet or more into the sky. Having tilled rich mineral subsoils for millennia, their roots now hunched up like gargantuan crab legs or sprawled out like gargantuan serpents. On the ground was a seemingly endless cushion of moss, squishing at my every footfall. Not content to cover only the ground, this moss crawled up the trunks of trees, too. From the branches of these same trees dangled a wispy green lichen called old man's beard—a fitting complement, I thought, to an old-growth forest.

The fog lent a spectral quality to a world that was already stranger, much stranger than the one I'd left behind. At any moment I expected to run into a *gaghit*. In Haida lore gaghits are demented, vaguely supernatural beings who inhabit the deepest, darkest parts of the forest. They can be easily identified by the sea urchin spines in their cheeks, wide nostrils that flare dramatically skyward, and their very long, very sharp fingernails. Gaghits specialize in the kidnapping of children; and while not exactly a child myself I couldn't help wondering whether an overly zealous gaghit might forego the splitting of hairs as to my classification.

Instead of a gaghit, however, I kept encountering fallen trees. They were everywhere, askew, aslant, and horizontal; they combined with ranks of dead snags to make my hike mainly an act of circumnavigation. At one point, more or less lost, I stopped to check my compass. And directly in front of me, moss-ridden, tapered at both ends, rotting but still distinct, lay an old Haida canoe at least thirty or forty feet in length.

An astounding discovery! I stood in the rain, no longer hearing its persistent drip-drip-drip, and stared at this mossy relic. Once upon a time the Haida had paddled canoes similar to it as far north as Alaska, as far south as California, and maybe even as far west as China. Such canoes, piled high with sea otter pelts, bobbed year after year alongside New England trading sloops, until the sea otter was virtually extinct in these waters. From mainland trade fairs they'd return filled with *eulachons,* a fish so rich in oil that a wick run through it will produce an instant lantern. They'd be used as ceremonial food platters at feasts and potlatches. And a canoe might even end up in a person's chest, whereupon a *nang sraagaa* (shaman) would be called in to exorcise it with a mystical massage.

But this particular canoe had never known the taste of seawater. It was at once dead, unborn, and derelict. I wondered how long it had rested here, untouched by human hands and unseen by human eyes, illuminated only by the green, subaquaceous Pacific light. And why was it left unfinished? Had a flaw in the grain been discovered as it was being worked to completion? Or did the smallpox epidemic that ravaged these islands in the last century ravage its carver too? The only answer to my questions was the sonorous *c-r-r-u-u-k* of a raven in a nearby tree. Or maybe it wasn't a raven, but Raven himself, trickster-transformer of northwest coast legend. Raven created or stole—it was all the same to him—sunlight, trees, fish, water, dirt, and even sex. He also created the people who created this canoe. Or so the story goes.

⪼◆⪻

Other Haida stories tell of cruel and unusual punishments suffered by those who do not respect Nature and its denizens. A woman makes fun of a dogfish because it has two penises, and slowly begins to turn into a dogfish herself. Two boys wantonly break the wings of bufflehead ducks and end up transformed into killer whales. A young man throws a live frog into the fire; a volcano erupts and destroys his village, killing everyone except an old woman and her granddaughter, both of whom had expressed sympathy for the frog.

Not surprisingly, I took care not to squash, crunch, or ridicule local fauna on my walk back through the woods. But I did mutter silent imprecations against the rain, now coming down in heavy buckets. At last, somewhat liquefied, I sloshed into Windy Bay. After visiting the remains of a nineteenth-century Haida lodge, I took refuge inside a modern lodge, albeit of traditional cedar-plank, post-and-beam construction, built right next to the older one. I entered this lodge in a highly unorthodox manner—through the doorlike pupil of a huge eye painted on the outside.

Built in the mid-1980s, Blinking Eye House was used as a base by the Haida during their protest against logging in the southern Queen Charlottes. Over the years various logging companies had sheared away much of the islands' luxuriant growth—old growth, new growth, ancient conifers and upstart saplings—moving north to south and coming closer, ever closer to Haida traditional sites like Windy Bay. The Haida had occupied this increasingly shorn land for ten thousand or so years, back to the time of Raven himself. And they felt such a lengthy tenure gave them the right to call that land their own, their very own, and to evict tree-lopping intruders if they so desired.

At first the Haida protest seemed to fall on deaf ears. After all, the forest industry underpins British Columbia's economy. So the province tends to take a dim view of those who bite the hand that ostensibly feeds them, even if that hand, in addition to feeding them, is messing up their environment. Never mind that logging can upset a rainforest's delicate nutrient and hydrological cycles and smother equally delicate aquatic habitats with bark and other debris; or that in its intensive, clearcut form it can turn a landscape into a desolation of jagged stumps, craterlike holes, and crumpled earth. Never mind, indeed, when a single old-growth tree equals the equivalent in board feet of five large houses.

As I huddled inside Blinking Eye House, I imagined the richly-blanketed figures in the shadows, men and women, elders and youth, Eagle and Raven moieties, all dedicated to the salvation of their land from the chain saw. Some would be lamenting the loss of great cedars—the staff of Haida life—first on Talunkwan Island, just north of here, and now on Lyell Island itself. Others might be complaining about the rumble of logging trucks only a few miles from Windy Bay, an age-old silence violated. Still others might be talking about the arrest of 72 protestors who'd blocked a logging road at Sedgwick Bay in 1985. Or in hushed tones describing how one of the protestors, an elder named Ada Jones, opened her Bible and read this passage just before the police led her away: "I have fought the good fight, I have finished the course. I have kept the faith."

If this were a Haida myth, the loggers might be transformed into ancient cedars. So too would the provincial officials who enforced the wielding of chain saws in Haida land. But it isn't a myth. On the other hand, a significant transformation did take place on July 11, 1987, mostly as a result of national support for the Haida. On that date British Columbia Prime Minister Bill Vander Zalm and Canadian Premiere Brian Mulroney signed a "Memorandum of Understanding" that led to the establishment of South Moresby National Park Reserve (any Canadian park subject to native land claims is called a reserve). Then another transformation occurred a few years later—the new park's name was changed to Gwaii Haanas, a name more in keeping with its wondrous aspect. More in keeping with its Haida aspect, too.

Even though logging was halted, the Haida were still not satisfied. After all, they'd never given away or sold this land, much less earmarked it for later use as a national park. So they forced the signing, on July 30, 1993, of the so-called Gwaii Haanas Agreement. This Agreement gives the Haida a role equal to the Canadian Crown's in the administration of Gwaii Haanas. And in doing so it creates an essential second line of defense—from the Tangil Peninsula south to Cape St. James—against the scorning of Nature and its denizens.

———◆———

Day after day, the *Kingii* nudged along the sheltered lee side of Gwaii Haanas, past islands with names like Huxley, Banks, Darwin, Faraday, Ramsay, and Murchison. Visiting the Queen Charlottes in the late 1870s, explorer-geologist George Dawson borrowed these names—all of which belonged to prominent nineteenth-century British scientists—and bestowed them on the local landscape in a manner not unlike a man flinging confetti. But at least one of the names, Darwin's, is appropriate for an archipelago often referred to as "the Canadian Galapagos." Mosses, liverworts, flowers, amphipods, birds, and fish are found here and nowhere else in the world. Or if they happen to be found elsewhere, they're found in the most improbable of places, such as the liverwort *Bendrobazzania griffithiana,* which occurs only in the Queen Charlottes and the Kingdom of Bhutan.

If asked to name one of these islands myself, I might have named it after some eminent ornithologist. Or I might have skipped the eminence and named it after one of the multitude of birds we encountered day and night during the trip. Bald eagles were everywhere, peering down at us from their lofty treetop aeries. Endless squadrons of black oyster-catchers would fly past us and begin pip-pipping hysterically, as if we'd committed some horrible outrage. Once in a while a horned puffin would fly by and then turn its head as if in amazement at a fellow creature so weirdly constituted as to possess radar and a mast. There were ancient murrelets, rhinoceros auklets, Cassin's auklets, pigeon guillemots, fork-winged petrels, green-winged teals, red-breasted mergansers, red-necked grebes, pied-billed grebes, black-footed albatrosses, oldsquaws, and marbled murrelets. The nesting site of this last bird—high up in old-growth trees—was a mystery until as recently as 1974, when a British Columbia tree surgeon accidentally knocked a marbled murrelet chick 138 feet to the ground.

At night I would camp ashore in moss-covered glades that were like topiaries run to riot. There I would be serenaded by the hammerlike sounds of hairy woodpeckers foraging in dead trees.

Or be awakened from my sleep by the loud squawks of ancient murrelets and rhinoceros auklets bonking themselves on the old growth, falling to the ground, then trying to fly and bonking themselves again. These birds head back to their burrows at night in order to avoid raptors like eagles and peregrine falcons. But their night vision is not nearly as sharp as their day vision. Nor are they designed to fly in such a despairing entanglement of forest. So they attempt to make direct hits on their burrows, an act they invariably fail at, not being designed for sudden landings, either. But such seemingly bumbling behavior at least keeps them from being the main course of an eagle's dinner.

One day the *Kingii* ploughed into an enormous raft of sooty shearwaters in Hecate Strait, the shallow body of water which separates the Queen Charlottes from the mainland. The shearwaters had dined not wisely but too well on krill and were now so heavy that they couldn't take off. As I watched these avian obesities flap their wings helplessly, I noticed the water pulse and boil, then become silvery. A school of herring was also attracted by the krill. Then geysers of spume announced the arrival of a pod of humpback whales. Soon the humpbacks were frolicking, leaping, diving, and swiveling, apparently unaware that it's bad manners to play with one's food. Their mouths, when they opened them, were literally red with krill. One whale seemed to wink its eye in my direction, as if to say: Quite a show we're putting on, isn't it?

Near Murchison Island we dropped anchor in a forest of lush golden kelp. Below the boat lay a sea that bloomed like the tropics, fueled by the interaction of the cold, nutrient-rich Pacific with slightly less cold, even more nutrient-rich waters closer to shore. Opalescent nudibranchs floated in slow motion like pieces of intricate jewelry liberated from their earthbound coffers. Anemones wriggled their finespun plumes to the rhythms of the tide. Stippled red crabs skittered back and forth along tongues of kelp as if on missions of the utmost importance. Starfish came in such a variety of colors—dark blues and purples, reds and browns, yellows and oranges—that they seemed to be competing with each other in some sort of intertidal beauty contest. I observed one even more flagrantly purple than the rest and reached down to pick it up. Try as I might, I couldn't pry it loose from its rocky home. Later I learned that this species of starfish can withstand a hundred-pound pull.

Kingii is Haida for "Always looking down in the water." Which describes exactly what we did for the next couple of hours. Terry and Charlotte Husband, the boat's co-skippers, waded around in search of rock scallops, while I gathered a bucket of sea urchins, chitons, turban snails, and mussels. Then Terry dug a two-foot-deep hole in the sand from which he managed to extricate a geoduck, a bivalve so fleshy that it can't retreat into its own shell. And that evening we sat down to an all-mollusk supper. It was a meal so rich in energy-giving protein that, upon finishing it, I felt like seeking out a black bear—the Queen Charlottes have the world's largest—and wrestling it into submission.

In fact, I had my chance with a bear the following day. I'd been searching for, hope against hope, a marbled murrelet's nest near De la Beche Inlet. A mile or so inland I ducked under a spruce log, and then I found myself face to face with a bear seated happily in a berry patch. Both of us did double takes, just like a pair of comics in the movies. Then I backed quickly under the log; the bear itself crashed off into the bush. A while later I figured that enough time had passed and the bear would be safely gone, so I stooped under the log again (it lay directly across the path). I came out on the other side just as the bear was returning to its former spot. We performed a second set of double takes, then I retreated a second time. But rather than risk a third rendezvous, I now made my way back to the boat. For I had a strong suspicion that an otherwise docile animal might not appreciate this sort of silliness. And it might show its lack of appreciation by wrestling *me* into submission.

At Hotspring Island I found myself in hot water again. Literal hot water. The island's eponymous springs boast temperatures that range from 89°F to 170°F. Settling into one of them, I entered a state of parboiled bliss. Several minutes later I was joined by the Haida Gwaii Watchman who was the island's caretaker. We sat there silently until I happened to mention the half-finished canoe I'd discovered in the Windy Bay watershed. The Watchman told me about finding a similar canoe himself a few years ago, on Burnaby Island. Then he added:

"You can't walk more than a couple of feet in Gwaii Haanas without stumbling on some trace of our past."

As the *Kingii* continued its journey, I began to realize that the Watchman's statement was not an exaggeration. At virtually every stream mouth or cove, I found old house pits, fire pits, lodge beams, bark-stripped trees, or fallen totem poles that had become nurse logs for future trees. Numerous shell middens proved that the Haida had used the same intertidal banquet table we'd used ourselves, only they took advantage of its year-round bounty for centuries.

Some of these sites would have been no more than seasonal camps. Others, like Tanu, were once substantial villages. In 1878, when George Dawson visited it, Tanu was the most flourishing settlement in the Queen Charlottes, with sixteen longhouses, each occupied by an extended family, and thirty totem poles rising above its wide, expansive beach. Then the smallpox epidemic struck (the Haida holocaust, it's been called, because it reduced the population by ninety percent). Seven years later the village was abandoned. And as I walked around what was left of it myself, accompanied by Wally Pollard, Tanu's Watchman, I could see only depressions in the ground and rotting timber. Tanu was too ruinous even to be called a ruin, too close to oblivion for my mind to reconstruct it.

Indeed, moss—the epidermis that covers all things both great and small in these parts—was already blurring the distinction between a human environment and a bryophitic one.

The same was true of Gwaii Haanas' non-Haida sites, which were no less ruinous, although considerably more recent, than the Haida ones. All that remained of Lockeport, a turn-of-the-century mining community and later a salmon cannery, was a battered trailer and a scattering of whiskey bottles. Rose Harbor's whaling station could be recognized only from its rusting boiler hulks and pier stumps. Collapsed 1960s hippie shacks lined the eastern shore of Burnaby Narrows. Ikeda, a thriving copper mining settlement between 1906 and 1920, was a ghost town; its grand hotel, a refurbished Yukon sternwheeler, had become an indeterminate corpse of wood and metal. At Jedway the only intact object I could locate was an old chamberpot chair standing forlornly in a spruce thicket. And Jedway Bay, a Japanese abalone cannery in the early 1930s, was a hodgepodge of rusted metal behind which stood a solitary gravemarker with the word *"Sayonara"* written on it—a perfect epitaph for all these deserted places.

And yet I did not find such places or even the Haida sites especially sad. Poignant, perhaps; but not sad. Rather, they seemed part of an enduring cycle by which Man born of Woman, or Woman born of Woman, has but a brief time—maybe a few years, maybe an eye-blink of centuries—on these bounteous shores. Then Nature will reassert itself, oxidizing metal, breaking down wood, and covering scars with a mantle of the richest green.

———◆———

At last we threaded the needle of Houston Stewart Channel and crossed several miles of open ocean to Anthony Island. Here was situated Sgan Gwaii, Red Cod Island Town, a place remarkable enough to be ranked with Egypt's pyramids and the Palace of

Versailles as a UNESCO World Heritage Site. And what a location for such a site! Anthony Island dangles on the edge of the continent, miles from the nearest town or city, seemingly poised to be swallowed up by the vast Pacific. Instead of swallowing it up, however, the Pacific often lashes it with winds in excess of 100 mph.

As we anchored a few hundred yards offshore, I studied this 395-acre tract of rock and Sitka spruce. Except for its wind-whipped and thus slightly tilted tree-line, it looked no different from most other islands on the west coast. But then Terry and I hopped into the zodiac, motored around a barrier island, and all at once sixteen totem poles stood silently before us like a row of exclamation points. A few were propped up by clamps and supports; several had ferns sprouting like cockades from their tops; a couple rested on pads of gravel; and all were bleached grey by the relentless elements. Even so, they had the appearance of sentinels from a distant era miraculously transported to the present.

And upon walking ashore I had the peculiar sensation of being watched by a bestiary of faces. There were eagles, black bears, grizzly bears, killer whales, beavers, and gigantic frogs. Some had bulging eyes and protruding tongues, others grimaced in decay, yet others were broken or crippled but still somehow capable of powerful scrutiny ... especially of a Gore-tex–clad oddity like myself. Not being chiseled from heroic cedar, I felt like an intruder on an intimate, totally private gathering.

Once upon a time this village of watchers had been the stronghold of the Kunghit, a band of southern Haida equally renowned for their artistic and warlike qualities. They would descend in a lightning raid on a village like Skidegate and then vanish into the fog, having taken men as slaves and women as wives. They'd also take scalps as trophies; and if there wasn't time to take a scalp, they'd simply take the entire head. Between 1785 and 1825 the Kunghit engaged in the maritime fur trade, benefiting greatly from their southerly location. From Yankee traders they acquired axes and adzes, possibly even block-and-tackle, tools which helped them give a monumental dimension to their totem poles and longhouses. Yet their culture, even as it prospered, was falling victim to the very influences that fed its prosperity. A social order that stretched back to the time of Raven began to collapse. Then smallpox struck. Ironically, when the last of the Kunghit left Sgan Gwaii in the 1870s and 1880s, they relocated to Skidegate, home of their former enemies.

The only surviving descendants of Sgan Gwaii are the poles themselves. Peering at their acrobatic columns of faces, I wondered what they betrayed of the Kunghit mind-set. Did they show pride, for instance? Or an aptitude for commerce? Or an aptitude for fierceness? Reflexively, my hand went to my scalp.

Wanegan, the site's Watchman, kept my imagination firmly in check. A bright, highly articulate man, he was a virtual encyclopedia of Haida lore. But even he found it hard to resist Sgan Gwaii's unusual ambience. He'd been coming here for more than twenty years, often by himself, although he confessed to me that he was never completely by himself—the ghosts of the past always seemed to hover nearby, going about their daily tasks, gathering shellfish, stripping bark, laughing, and occasionally even crying.

As we wandered from pole to pole, Wanegan explained that "totem pole" is actually a misnomer, at least as far as these particular poles were concerned. Most were mortuary poles. They were erected to honor a deceased family member or chief, whose remains—after a suitable period of mummification—would be packed into a carved cedar box and then put in a rectangular chamber at the very top of the pole. He pointed to a heap of bones thirty or so feet above my head. And as I looked up at these bones I couldn't help but think how satisfying it would be to enjoy one's eternal slumber perpetually aloft like this, close to family and longhouse.

The animals incised into the poles were not monsters or demons, Wanegan said. Nor were they deity figures whom the Haida worshipped, contrary to the opinion of early missionaries. Instead, they were exclusively held crests of social identity and rank, somewhat like a European coat-of-arms or a Scottish tartan. Crests of the Raven moiety included the raven, killer whale, grizzly bear, and mountain goat, while Eagle crests included the eagle, frog, and beaver. Each crest told a story about how the dead person gained the privilege of its use by his family's contact long ago with the animal itself.

"Can you tell me one of the stories?" I asked.

Wanegan shook his head. The stories had disappeared with the Kunghit themselves and were now lost, lost forever.

We approached the stumps of several poles that had been shipped off to museums and galleries some years ago. To Wanegan, this was not unlike wrenching a person from his home for no reason and then clamping him in jail. "Those poles were born in Sgan Gwaii," he declared. "They should be allowed to die here."

And the poles that remained were in fact dying here, slowly but surely dying here, buffeted by the wind, scoured by salt spray, and eaten by wood-boring insects. Many Haida think this is as it should be, since these skyscrapers of wood were not created to last forever—in the old days, when one of them toppled over, it was merely pushed aside, allowed to become one with the earth again.

It was now growing dark. I began walking away from the site, past the ruins of longhouses with names like Thunder Rolls Upon It House and People Think of This House Even When They Sleep Because the Master Feeds Everyone Who Calls. Before I climbed into the zodiac, I turned for one final look at the poles. They seemed almost human in the twilight, like stoic, elderly gentlemen who'd seen much, borne much, so I murmured a polite goodbye to them. There was no reply, not even the hint of a reply: only the faint whisper of wind in the Sitka spruce and the cry of a raven far, far away.

ISLANDS OFF
THE MAP

IN BANDA

Like most scrutable Occidentals, I tend to be a bundle of fallacies and clichés about the so-called inscrutable East. Something to do with Charlie Chan movies and overly generous doses of Dr. Fu Manchu at an impressionable age, I suspect. About Indonesia, however, I seem to have fewer stereotypes than I have about other Eastern places. Probably that's because island-rich Indonesia is not so much a single place as it is 13,667 distinct places, some so obscure they've fallen right off the map. Take the Banda Islands. When I informed a well-traveled friend that I was visiting Banda, he said:

"Hastings Banda? The doyen of discretionary nonalignment? The man's older than sin. Actually, I thought he was dead."

Whereupon I confessed that I wasn't visiting the President-for-Life of Malawi, but a group of small islands in the Moluccan archipelago in eastern Indonesia. Banda, I added, was stomping-ground for the *tjoelik*, a ghost whose specialty is nipping off peoples' heads, along with the *laweri*, a fish with a built-in flashlight.

"Ah, you old fantasist," my friend said. "Now I know you're making it all up. You *are* visiting Hastings Banda, aren't you?"

———

Shortly after this conversation, I hopped a series of increasingly smaller planes until I touched down on Neira, the capital island. Here in the flesh was a genuine Banda, quite obviously neither an aged African potentate or a figment of my imagination. Almost the first sight that greeted my eyes was a large crowd of locals gathered around an open-air TV; they were watching an old *I Love Lucy* rerun dubbed in Bahasa Indonesia, even as a muezzin's voice from a nearby mosque was inciting them to prayer.

Such an image suggests a cheerful little backwater wholly removed from the pulse of modern life. Maybe this image is true today, but the Bandas weren't always cheerful, nor were they always a backwater. No less a celebrity than Christopher Columbus may have even been searching for them when he discovered, much to his disappointment, America. And the usual roll-call of European empire builders—the Spanish, the Portuguese, the English, and the Dutch—all tried to colonize them at one time or another. At last the Dutch prevailed, largely through the efforts of a soldier-adventurer named Jan Pieterszoon Coen, who put to death every male Bandanese over the age of fifteen.

Why such interest in a bunch of remote, pinprick islands? Because the Bandas grew nutmeg, the "gold" of the spice trade, in astonishingly profuse groves. That this spice inspired the genocidal instincts of the normally mild-mannered Dutch is, I suppose, a tribute to its former versatility—it was used as a seasoning, a meat preservative, a source of mace, and a cure for madness and sciatica. Also, nutmeg is a mild hallucinogen, a fact presumably not lost on the sailors who were transporting it all the way back to Europe.

My first day on Neira I took a little stroll and noticed some curious reminders of the long-departed Dutch. Inside the old jail, there was a badly warped but still serviceable ping-pong table. There were tumbledown *perkenier* (planter) homesteads whose tiled floors had been invaded by poinciana trees and whose shallow marble steps were covered with maidenhair ferns: former stately mansions transformed into botanical displays. Then there were all those cannons—cannons by the roadside, cannons in gardens, cannons in tidal flats, and even one forlorn cannon still guarding the battlements of Fort Belgica. If nothing else, these slightly absurd relics showed how much easier it is to get rid of a colonial master than colonial ironmongery.

I was photographing a cannon that seemed to be growing in somebody's banana grove when a policeman approached me. Uh-oh, I thought, not three hours here and you're already in trouble with the local gendarmes. I'd heard stories about the Indonesian police casually jailing trespassers, jaywalkers, and other small-time felons, so I wondered if I was going to inaugurate my visit to Banda with a shakedown in the old jail. If that were the case, I decided I'd at least request a cellmate who played ping-pong. But this particular policeman simply asked me whether I'd like a banana. And before I could respond, he'd plucked down a ripe *pisang susu,* renowned for its milky flavor.

Later I wrote these words in my notebook: "Indonesia is a land of contrasts. In Timor the police machine-gun you. Here they offer you bananas."

⇒•◦•⇐

Taken together, the ten Banda Islands cover only twenty square miles of dry land, or roughly 1/25,000 the total area of Indonesia. The largest island, boomerang-shaped Lontar, is seven miles long and scarcely a mile wide; the smallest, Kapal, is a blunt outcropping of rock. Neira itself is small enough that even the most torpid walker can negotiate it in a few hours. Small wonder that cartographers occasionally turn their talents to more momentous places. On the other hand, if you remind yourself that the Bandas rise 22,000 feet sheer from the bottom of the Banda Sea, that they are in fact the merest tips of abyssal volcanoes, then they seem pretty momentous themselves.

Of all the Bandas, Gunung Api is the one most likely to resent being called a "tip," since its Fuji-like centerpiece, Fire Mountain, is a full-fledged, still active volcano, complete with a resident fire goddess, Pele, who reputedly has a more or less conjugal relationship with the mountain. It's also said that whenever any sort of invasion force arrives in Banda, she persuades the mountain to blow its top. In 1615, Fire Mountain erupted just as a Dutch fleet sailed into the strait between Gunung Api and Neira. It erupted again in the 1790s to mark the coming of an English expeditionary force. The most recent eruption, in May of 1988, forced a mass evacuation of Gunung Api and all the islands around it. There wasn't an invasion this time—not unless you consider a visit by Jacques Cousteau an invasion.

An ascent of Fire Mountain is almost an official act for the visitor, so I hired a guide named Ali to take me up and down this pyramid of living rock. Like many Bandanese, Ali was something of a demographic jumble; Dutch features fought Javanese and Arab trader features for supremacy on his face. For my purposes, he also happened to be the local equivalent of a Sherpa.

Ali and I started our ascent at 5:30 A.M. to keep from being fricasseed by the midday sun. We followed a path uphill that led through a dense nutmeg plantation. Immediately I began to hear the booming *"Aw-w-w, aw-w-w, aw-w-w"* of the nutmeg pigeon, a handsome, green-collared bird celebrated by Alfred Wallace in his classic travelogue *The Malay Archipelago,* but much disliked by the Bandanese themselves. Indeed, they dislike it so much that they represent it as the Bird of Death in their mythology. No doubt they'd make even the chickadee a Bird of Death if, like the pigeon, a single chickadee consumed a dozen or so nutmeg "nuts" a day.

The actual climb wasn't difficult. It was just that the human creature isn't accustomed to getting down on all fours and crawling up a slope of volcanic rubble like an early primate. But that's the only way to avoid sliding two steps backwards for every successful step forwards. Likewise it's the only way to avoid ending up with a souvenir imprint of lava on your person. The lack of interest in this sort of souvenir is probably why the first European ascent of Fire Mountain didn't occur until 1821, a relatively recent date.

At last we made it up to the summit, a place of smoking rock, barren and sulphurous, that reminded me a little of Iceland. But the view was distinctly not Icelandic—both the near Bandas and the far Bandas spread out on a sea so azure, so pellucid that it made every other sea seem dingy by comparison.

I asked Ali if he knew about Pele.

He nodded. "Sometimes we sacrifice a kitchen to her," he said.

"A kitchen? Hard to haul a whole kitchen up these slopes."

"Not hard, easy," he replied, adding: "We cut its throat, too."

"You cut the kitchen's throat?"

He nodded again. Just as I was about to ask him what type of knife he used, I realized: Indonesians pronounce "k" and "c" like "ch," so Ali naturally was pronouncing "ch" as if it were "k." It's much easier to cut a chicken's throat than a kitchen's.

We descended the same way we came up, slipping, sliding, and glissading over hardened lava from the 1988 eruption. Now and then I had to grab the branch of a nutmeg tree as a belay—another use for this versatile spice?—to keep from falling down. By the time I reached bottom, I felt I'd been participating in an illusion. True, Fire Mountain was only 2,100 feet tall, less than half the height of Denver, Colorado. Yet it had become incomparably large, even momentous under my feet, as if it'd been touched by magic.

———✦———

After my assault on Fire Mountain, I decided to spend a restful day exploring Bandanese waters in a *prahu*. A prahu is a dugout canoe made from the hollowed-out trunk of a tropical almond tree. With their narrow girths and unusually low-slung gunwales, prahus are better suited to the delicate Bandanese frame than the more cumbersome Western one. Or so the Bandanese man from whom I rented my prahu delicately put it. He also said I'd look funny. But that didn't bother me. Westerners are supposed to look funny in Indonesia. They talk funny, walk funny, and dress funny, too. Such has been our lot ever since the first European crept onto these sultry shores wearing garments that would not have been out of place in Greenland.

Right then and there I tried to launch my craft. "Slowly, slowly," the owner told me, lest I capsize the prahu even before I got into it. Somehow I did manage to get into it (to balance yourself in a prahu, I'm convinced, requires divine intervention) and was soon paddling, after a fashion, in the general direction of Lontar. Fishermen stared at me from their prahus. Small children stared at me from theirs. And I stared right back at them as if I knew exactly what I was doing. I didn't, of course. Despite some familiarity with canoes, I wasn't prepared for this lighter-than-air craft, which the daintiest of starboard strokes would send rushing off toward Irian Jaya. Or with an equally dainty port stroke, it'd rush off toward Singapore.

Finally I found the solution to my problems: a constant use of the J stroke. This kept me from zigzagging furiously, traveling in a circle, or making my landfall in the wrong country. As I paddled around Neira's southern tip, I thought I was doing quite well. Then I noticed a grizzled old woman shoot right past me in her prahu. My self-esteem vanished. But here I ought to mention that women, especially elderly women, are known as the best paddlers in Banda and always seem to be in considerable demand as seagoing chauffeurs.

Before long, I was approaching Lontar's southern coast. Never mind that I'd been aiming for Salomon Beach on its northern coast.

At least I'd kept myself away from Singapore. Now I began to wonder what the good people of Lontar would think when I fetched up on their island in one of their own eminently capsizable crafts. I found out soon enough. For after the prahu struck bottom, I made what I thought was an elegant leap ashore and landed face down in Lontar's rich volcanic sand. Well, partially sand and partially mud. The welcoming committee of children and young adults burst into riotous laughter. Funny Westerner! They slapped their knees and rolled in the mud, too.

Then a man in a fez stepped forward and invited me to his home for a cup of tea. I assumed he just wanted a private performance of my comic routine. Actually, this man had no such interest at all. He was the local schoolteacher and he'd been looking for someone on whom to practice his English for quite some time. Whatever my defects in canoemanship, I seemed to be that person. So we went back to his house, a small bungalow with a slatted driftwood floor and sago-thatch roof. Here lived his entire family, including his seven children, all of whom slept in the same room. Apparently the parents slept in this not very spacious room, too.

Very crowded, I remarked. Oh, not crowded at all, the man replied. And then with a tolerant smile (Naive Westerner!), he said: "Banda people like to sleep this way. It is very good to sleep this way. For if a person sleeps alone and he has a nightmare, who would comfort him?"

———— ❧ ————

Whereas Neira, Lontar, and Gunung Api hunch together like three old comrades in an attitude of reminiscence, the islands of Ai, Hatta, and Rhun are distant and farflung, less like comrades than mortal enemies. Rhun, the least comradely, most farflung of the three, is a nutmeg jungle fringed by a tracery of palm trees. Under the 1667 Treaty of Breda, the English gave the Dutch this tidbit of real estate—the only Banda they still clung to—in exchange for the then equally obscure island of Manhattan, in the Americas. A somewhat lopsided trade at that time: Manhattan's nutmeg was nonexistent.

For several days I'd wanted to visit Rhun, but the vagrant winds of the western monsoon kept interfering with my plans. At last there came a day of almost celestial calm, and off I went with a couple of Australian divers. They wanted to look at Rhun from under the water; I wanted to see the island's terrestrial realm and compare it with Manhattan's. The two-and-a-half-hour boat journey passed without incident until one of the Australians started trolling and a sea-eagle swooped down dramatically from the sky and snatched his artificial lure. Suddenly, he had an eagle at the end of his hook.

We landed on a deserted beach. The very next moment this same beach was swarming with a boisterous mass of people eager to see the Westerners. On Manhattan, they mug you; on Rhun, they mob you as if you were equal parts visiting dignitary, prize orchid, and two-headed calf. Our mob followed us through the village to the house of the *orang besar* (headman), piling in until the room where we were received by this cordial gentleman came to resemble the famous stateroom scene in the Marx Brothers' *A Night at the Opera*.

"How many people live on your island?" one of the Australians asked the orang besar.

"Forty-nine grandfathers," he answered proudly.

After the Australians left, the orang besar told me about an old English fort, El Dorado, which was the one possible tourist site on Rhun. He drew me up a map, and I headed back through the village with a parade of barefoot children running ahead of, alongside, and behind me. A bit slower, but also barefoot, was one of Rhun's forty-nine grandfathers; he was in a *sopi* (palm wine) haze and wondered if I'd come here to reclaim his island for the English ...

LAWRENCE MILLMAN

"English!" shrieked one of the kids. And as if this were his cue, he began the ubiquitous practice of English on me. "What your name, mister?" "You have wife, mister?" "Where you from, mister?" Along with other Indonesians, the Bandanese call all Westerners, including women, "mister"—a survival from colonial times when they were obliged to call Dutchmen "Mynheer."

"I'm from America," I told the kid.

"Is it a big or a little island?"

"A big, big island..."

Now I paused to rest from the heat. I sat down and opened my copy of Somerset Maugham's *The Narrow Corner,* a novel set in a fictionalized Banda. My escorts paused to rest, too. They sat down inches from my book and stared at it as if it were the world's greatest curiosity. When I turned it upside down, they continued to stare at it, but also stared back at me. Ah, he reads upside down, maybe they were telling themselves: Another insight into the baffling ways of Westerners.

And then I was following a path through the aromatic bush. I passed gay, flitting butterflies with seven-inch wingspans, brilliant orange spiders, and a marsupial cuscus asleep in a nutmeg tree. Finally I reached El Dorado. The fort turned out to be little more than a heap of crumbling stones, even worse off than the planters' houses on Neira. So much for Rhun's entry into the Taj Mahal or Parthenon sweepstakes. But it's the journey, not the destination, that matters most. And I did happen to notice a lovely polka-dotted butterfly resting its wings on one of the crumbling stones.

Back on Neira I got into a chat with Des Alwi, a son of Banda who'd made good as a diplomat, filmmaker, and local hotelier. If the Dutch hadn't traded Manhattan for Rhun, Alwi told me with a sly grin, the whole course of American history might have been different. Perhaps I might have been different, too—a devotee of Queen Beatrix and wooden shoes instead of apple pie.

"But I'm 'different' already," I protested, citing my high degree of exoticism for the Rhun-ites.

————▸•◂————

Where was I? Bent over the side of a small boat just off the north shore of Neira. It was a placid, star-filled night, and I was scouring the water for a very special fish. I'd already seen plenty of other fish on this trip—electric-blue, jade-green, and baby-pink fish, a teeming kaleidoscope of color. I'd also seen fish with spikes sticking out of their heads, fish that seemed to be dressed in tuxedos, and fish whose poison glands were fully capable of delivering me to an early grave. But these were all fish that could be found in any well-stocked reef in Asia or the Pacific. My fish was a Banda fish, occurring nowhere else but in the prodigal waters off of Banda itself.

I refer to the laweri (*Photoblepheron bandanensis*), locally known as "the flashlight fish." The laweri has an organ just below the eyes which enables it to light up its own field of vision. This organ goes on shining even after the fish itself is dead, so the Bandanese often take a couple of laweris, stick them in a jar, and they've got an instant night-light. Or if they're fishing in deep water, they might put a laweri at the end of a line and it'll illuminate the bait for fish not quite so remarkably endowed in the ocular department.

Suddenly the boatman gave a shout. He pointed to a small pool of light, at once ghostly and radiant, moving in the water. Several small pools of light. Laweris! These must have been five-watt laweris, since their light was a trifle weak. Then, off in the distance, I saw a group of much larger pools, definitely the twenty-watt variety, swimming briskly as a single unit. As they approached us, the entire sea came alive, shimmered, and gleamed with their presence.

And then they were gone. Once again the water was black as pitch. The only light in all the world came from flickering stars and the boatman's cigarette. But this encounter, so haunting, so altogether unusual, stayed with me long after I hopped that series of increasingly larger planes home. It stays with me even now, as I sit at my desk and write these words, illuminated by an ordinary, slightly boring light bulb.

TINY KINGDOM
BY THE SEA

✼

One day on Sark I found myself chatting with an elderly woman who looked like a French peasant and even spoke a sixteenth-century Norman-French *patois*. She switched to English for my benefit, then told me about the local custom (now, alas!, discontinued) of informing the bees in the event of a death in the family. You knocked on their hive and whispered all the pertinent details to them. If you failed to do this, or if your tone of voice was a wee bit too flippant, your bees would all fly away and leave you with a derelict hive.

"Why bees?" I asked. "Why not sheep? Why not cows? Why not tourists, in fact?"

"Tourists are not beautiful," the woman replied. "Bees, on Sark, are beautiful."

———•◦•———

Eight miles east of Guernsey, the isle of Sark is part of Britain even though it does not always feel British. Sometimes, of course, it feels very British, and then you think you've stumbled on a marriage of beetling Cornish cliffs with the honeysuckle hedgerows of Kent. Other times there seems to be an entirely different marriage, as between Never-Never Land and some cloud cuckoo version of France, with a dash of Ionesco thrown in for good measure. This latter marriage suggests a sort of Bhutan of the English Channel. For Sark is, or claims to be, the last true bastion of feudalism in a Britain increasingly done in by income tax, VAT, and death duties, none of which the island itself possesses.

At least part of Sark's feudalism is not really feudal at all. It's simply a refusal to genuflect before that much-adored modern deity, the motor car. By decree of the late Dame, Sibyl Hathaway, who ruled Sark with an iron hand for forty-seven years, only tractors could grace the island's unpaved roads—and then only if they proceeded at no more accelerated a speed than a policeman can walk. But shortly after this decree, she seemed to relent, and a Land Rover was allowed ashore. The island Parliament, Chief Pleas, was aghast. Then they realized that the Dame thought a Land Rover was some sort of glorified Boy Scout. More typical was the fate of the Citroën 2CV recently used in the filming of Mervyn Peake's novel about Sark, *Mr. Pye.* Upon arrival the key and distributor cap were removed, and it was trundled about behind a tractor.

I must confess that I'm no great admirer of automobiles myself. You can't chat about bees with them, can't break bread with them, can't even milk them. What possible use can they serve besides squashing the occasional nasty child? The only person I met on Sark who wanted one of these inhuman conveyances turned out to be the local village idiot, dribble-powered but fortunately not petrol-powered. Most of the non-idiots I encountered believed that cars would ravish the island's quietude like a fleet of Attila's Huns. And not just its quietude, but also its relatively unadulterated air—Sark air contains only one part per million carbon monoxide, whereas there are twenty parts per million at Smithfield Market, London.

How, then, does the visitor "see" Sark? By bicycle or, even better, shank's mare. I would not recommend a seat on a governess cart, leather-hooded victoria, or waggonette. Scores of day-trippers arrive from the other Channel Islands and get a whirlwind tour in one of these rather too cute carriages, driven by horsestruck young ladies from the English Midlands. But as banks and hedges are high and the best parts of the island inaccessible by wheeled vehicle, most of these day-trippers come away wondering what sort of experience, if any, they've had. Sark yields its secrets gradually, almost begrudgingly. After a week there myself, I still had not seen any of the island's myriad ghosts, including the Grey Lady of Dixcart Valley, whom I especially wanted to see because she was supposed to be quite beautiful...

<hr />

Sark is small—only 4½ square miles. But it has such an assortment of headlands, coves, and gnawing intrusions by the sea that it often seems without limits or boundaries, a place altogether at odds with its cozy reputation. That bramble-covered cliff might be a fifteen-minute walk away, or an hour. That path, which starts out so straight, switches back on itself and thus requires a genuine hike, not a casual stroll.

Actually, there are two Sarks, Big and Little, joined together by a lofty isthmus (an excellent place for a suicide, locals boast) called The Coupée. And to hear the inhabitants of Little Sark discuss Big Sark, where most of the commerce is, you'd think they were talking about a damaged civilization on the other side of the globe rather than a kindred chunk of granite a few hundred yards away.

The guidebooks try to make a case for the island's few obvious tourist attractions. They recommend a visit to an old windmill decapitated by the Germans during the Occupation. Or they suggest a visit to one of the world's smallest jails, but warn you not to get caught with drugs on your person or you'll end up visiting it more intimately than you expect.

Well, decapitated windmills and closet-sized jails are nice, but Sark's meandering paths are much nicer. Once you get yourself on one of them, even the island's antiquated bustle seems to vanish. You're alone in a world where the screeches of kittiwakes and the crisp rustle of cattle munching the short grass are the only sounds; a world of rock and color, and forest lanes often preposterously green.

There are paths to yawning holes in the earth like Creux Derrible, where the sea pounds and sucks a hundred feet below you. There are paths that take you to raised beaches, and paths that take you to beaches that aren't raised. There are paths along Little Sark's bared granite, and paths that wind through deep, lush valleys of primrose and wild hyacinth. There are paths that seem like little more than precipitous steps etched into a cliffside, and paths so dusty that a false step will deposit you among the prickles of a gorse bush. There are gentle paths and rough paths and paths that seem to meander aimlessly through carpets of buttercups and marigolds, flowers that impart to Sark butter its unusually bright color.

My favorite path was located on the eastern rim of Little Sark. It descended past a disused copper mine to an isolated, anemone-rich cove called Pot Bay. Here I'd sit by myself every afternoon and jot notes in my journal. One afternoon I climbed down this path, now clasping the iron handrail, now the rope generously placed alongside it. Halfway down I slipped and fell into, yes, an eagerly awaiting gorse bush. At last I reached the bottom and saw that I was not alone, after all. A man and woman of somewhat advanced years were engaged in the popular British pastime of sunning themselves in a thick overcast. Both of them were sprawled on beach towels, and both were extremely naked.

"We're nudists," the man announced to me, a bit unnecessarily, I thought.

"We've been going naked for thirty-eight years," the woman said proudly, adding: "We always spend our holidays by the sea."

"By the way, what do you say to a cup of tea, guv'nor?" the man asked me, removing a thermos from his kit bag and putting some cups on a makeshift sandstone table.

And so I ended up having afternoon tea in the primal arena of Pot Bay with these pink, blithe souls. Only on Sark, I remember thinking.

———✦———

If Sark is Britain's last feudal stronghold, then Michael Beaumont is its last real feudal lord. A former aeronautical engineer, Mr. Beaumont became Le Seigneur of Sark in 1974 upon the death of his grandmother, the Dame. He holds the island, its lands and all its diverse paths, in permanent lease from the Crown, to which he pays an annual rent of £2.50. That's a not significantly higher sum than Sark's first colonizer, a Jersey nobleman named Helier de Carteret, paid a much earlier Queen Elizabeth. As Seigneur, Mr. Beaumont has exclusive right to raise doves and keep an unspayed bitch. He receives one-thirteenth of the profits from all land sales and can claim a chimney tax—one chicken per chimney annually—from every island householder if he so desires.

I decided to visit Mr. Beaumont and offer him my fealty as a fellow devotee of cheerful anachronisms. But I wanted to learn a little about the workings of his kingdom, too. So I set up an appointment with him and, arriving a bit early for it, took a stroll around the Seignerie's capacious grounds. I noticed a cannon which bore this inscription: *Don de Sa Majesté la Royne Elizabeth au Seigneur du Serq A.D. 1572.* I also saw an old chapel now being used to store gardening equipment, a perfectly splendid solution, it seemed to me, for what to do with an idle House of God on your property.

Mr. Beaumont received me in the Seignerie's parlor. I'd dressed formally for the occasion; he was wearing a sweatshirt, a pair of ragged shorts, and sneakers. It was obvious that he'd rather be digging around in his garden, one of the Channel Islands' finest, than talking with another (another!) journalist. And who could blame him?

I began by asking him if he'd deported any unsavory characters lately, as this was one of his Seignorial rights.

No, he said. It might be well within his right, but nowadays you can't go around deporting people, however unsavory they are, for fear of litigation.

Then I asked whether he'd ever benefited from the custom of *droit du seigneur,* by which a bride is obliged to sleep with the lord of the manor on her wedding night.

No, droit du seigneur was never practiced on Sark, he said, noting, however, that journalists never fail to ask him about it.

Well, I said, have you received your due in chickens yet?

He shook his head. Most of his feudal dues had long been scrapped in favor of high excise duties on alcohol, tobacco, and tourists. But there was a staunchly feudal survival on Sark, he said, and a very good survival it was, too. That was the system of land tenure. Tradition required that all land pass from father to first-born son. Furthermore, no land could ever be subdivided. Any outsider who wished to purchase a piece of Sark could do so only if he'd lived on the island for a minimum of ten years, and then only if that piece of Sark hadn't already been designated as agricultural land. This kept the island from becoming a suburbanized resort like Guernsey or Jersey. It also kept the majority of tax exiles at arm's, if not ocean's, length.

"Really," said Mr. Beaumont, "all we want is to carry on in our own sweet little way."

He was smiling, yet I think I detected in that smile a special plea for his island and perhaps all small, plodding, infinitely fragile islands everywhere. A plea that said: Look, but don't touch. Traveler, pass on.

———⇒•⇐———

Toward the end of my trip I found myself chatting with a Sark farmer, a man who'd milked so many cows in his day that he was now permanently bent into the posture of milking a cow. All of a sudden there was a rustling in the brush. A jet-black cat emerged, looked around, and quickly retreated to the brush. Or at least it seemed an animal with the attributes, including a certain feline grace, of a cat.

"Yours?" I asked the farmer. He laughed a deep throaty laugh and said it wasn't a cat, no, not even remotely a cat, but rather a black rat, a species found here to the exclusion of the common brown variety. I was surprised, to put it mildly, and not a little embarrassed at my blunder.

On Sark, even the rats are beautiful.

SECRET ISLAND
OF THE GULF

✤

"I don't even know what street Canada is on," Al Capone reputedly scoffed when one of his cronies suggested that he include our northern neighbor in his empire of crime.

On what street, I wonder, would he have put Anticosti?

This Quebec island, which plugs the Gulf of St. Lawrence like a huge cucumber, is one-third larger than Prince Edward Island, yet people far more geographically literate than Al Capone don't know that it exists. I first read about it myself in a genuinely awful novel, *The Confessions of Con Cregan,* by the nineteenth-century Irish novelist Charles Lever. Rainbound in a West Kerry guesthouse, I had only Lever's novel and a Gaelic Bible as reading material. I chose the novel and ended up ploughing through page after page of overwrought prose about an island ruled by a crazed mulatto sailor. This sailor would rob shipwreck victims and occasionally eat them, too. I confess that I didn't find this too inviting, culinarily or otherwise. On the other hand, I was very curious about the island, an obscure chunk of land closer to my New England doorstep than Al Capone's home town of Chicago.

Most of Anticosti's relatively few visitors are deer hunters and salmon fishermen. But even they seem not to have heard of the island. They fly in, bag their deer or fish, and then fly out again without ever seeing Vauréal Canyon or the lyrical meadows of Baie Ste. Claire. My well-traveled friends hadn't heard of Anticosti, either. When I told one of them that I was going there, he promptly confused it with the Azores and asked me to drink a bottle of hearty Portuguese wine for him.

My friend wasn't alone in his confusion. Starting with Jacques Cartier, who mistook Anticosti's largest river, the Jupiter, for the Northwest Passage, the island has invariably been fertile ground for error. Early visitors believed its trees were bunched so closely together that you couldn't walk through them but had to walk on top of them. And early mariners thought its fogs so persistent that sometimes years would pass without anyone actually seeing the island.

Anticosti has been fertile ground for dashed hopes, too. Tiny cemeteries sprinkle the island's shores, with lonely gravemarkers half-hidden by bush and worn by the weather, memorializing ... who? What anonymous people from which century? Rusting shipwrecks, abandoned lighthouses, and logging roads that lead nowhere—all are mute testimony to the vanity of human wishes.

The ghost villages of Fox Bay, Anse aux Fraises, and Baie Ste. Claire testify to the vanity of human settlement. One such attempt at settlement, by the so-called Anticosti Company, was notable for the stock of supplies sent up from Montreal: six crates of violin strings, a case of coffin handles, a thousand steel bars, a box of trout flies, and a couple of English saddles. Not surprisingly, the settlers went home the first chance they got.

And then there was Henri Menier, the Chocolate King of France. In 1895, he bought Anticosti with profits from his chocolate firm, then proceeded to run the island more or less as an independent feudal country, with his hunting and fishing requirements the sole industry. As his seigniory, he built a part Norman, part

LAWRENCE MILLMAN

Viking chateau complete with world-class wine cellar, Baccarat crystal, and a three-story fleur-de-lis window. So brightly illuminated was this fleur-de-lis at night that a good many seafarers must have taken one look at it and wondered whether they'd made a serious navigational error: Was this the Gulf of St. Lawrence, or was it perhaps the coast of France? Menier also imported a veritable bestiary to the island—beaver, moose, reindeer, elk, buffalo, rabbits, frogs, and 220 white-tailed Virginia deer.

But even the Chocolate King could not tame Anticosti. His legacy consists of the animals, along with the somewhat immodest name, Port-Menier, that he gave to his "capital." The rest is history. It's as if the island possessed its own ecological gods, silent denizens of the softwood forests and limestone cliffs, who protect it from development. It is a place nearly as wild today as it was on the day in 1534 when Jacques Cartier mistook one of its peat bogs for potentially rich farmland.

———◦◦◦———

Yet Anticosti is not hostile to visitors. It merely asks the visitor to accept it on its own idiosyncratic terms. Consider the roads. In one sense, they're among the worst roads I've ever had the pleasure of driving on. But in another sense they're roads like the roads our grandfathers used to make, *real* roads, not effete asphalt imitations. They boast tooth-loosening gravel, classic washboarding, and potholes seemingly deep enough to swallow a vehicle forever. They insist that you move slowly in order to notice the bald eagles riding the thermals overhead or the rivers meandering along beside you, some an azure color, others cappuccino, and at least one river—the Jupiter—an exotic shade of neon turquoise.

On these roads, you won't find motorists sniffing each other's tails like a conga line of dogs in heat. Just the opposite, in fact. One day I drove from my digs at Carleton to Cape Sandtop, five hours in all, and I didn't see another vehicle. Not a single battered pickup in well over a hundred miles. That in itself is a sightseeing attraction for anyone suffering from traffic burnout.

I did see deer, however. On and off the road, browsing or staring at me, they were everywhere. At one point I stopped to investigate a giant red-capped mushroom, and a virtual sea of bobbing white tails disappeared into a frieze of spruce and balsam fir. All thanks to Monsieur Menier for this sight: his original herd now numbers 125,000, more per square mile than anywhere else in Canada. Woody Allen, mortally afraid of deer, would not like it here.

As for the deer themselves, they need a creature to be mortally afraid of. There are simply too many of them. Maybe SEPAQ, the Quebec crown corporation which manages Anticosti, should introduce mountain lions or grey wolves to the island. These honest predators would not limit their kill to trophy bucks, but would kill democratically, young bucks and old, does, and even cute little fawns. And this would bring down the deer population, not to mention giving the aforesaid predators, long out of work, a job.

———⇒•⇐———

Anticosti is an ancient seabed, pushed up and only slightly modified for terrestrial purposes. It has no mountains and practically no hills, which gives its vistas a grandeur not unlike the Big Sky country of Montana ... except when those vistas are obstructed by primevally thick forests. Then the island suggests an older, much older New England, before the advent of clearcutting, before the arrival of Europeans, perhaps even before the Indians.

To explore the island, you need to look low instead of high and down instead of up. And one day near Lake Wickenden I happened to look down, only to find myself standing in Silurian Park, a prehistoric habitat considerably less menacing than its Jurassic counterpart. At my feet was an outcropping of limestone literally studded with marine fossils. It contained vertebrae-like crinoids, brachiopods, and especially rugoses, a solitary, horn-shaped coral that covered the bottom of Silurian seas. I felt humbled. For this was a place old beyond my comprehension, a place whose years were reckoned not in the thousands, not in the millions, but in the hundreds of millions.

Another day I walked down into Vauréal Canyon, formerly Motherall Canyon, but renamed by Menier after his estate in France. Earlier that day a little flirt of snow had reminded me of just how far north I was. But now the weather was almost Mediterranean, with a sky like soft blue parchment. By the time I reached the canyon floor, I was genuinely hot from a mixture of sun and sun-blessed rock.

Now I began following the Vauréal River upstream. On either side of me, rising up at a near-vertical pitch, were steep grey walls that seemed to be made of old elephant hide. The dusky river itself, hardly more than a trickle, seemed to be made of Scotch broth. And except for this river, there was no movement or sound anywhere. I felt as if I'd descended through the earth's crust to its benthic core.

Each time the canyon turned and turned on itself again, I half expected to meet a knot of camera-wielding tourists recently expelled from a tour bus. A Grand Canyon reflex, I suppose. But in Vauréal Canyon the only living thing I encountered was a white-throated sparrow, whose high-pitched song—*O sweet Canada, Canada, Canada*—serenaded me onward. At last I came to the canyon's *pièce de résistance,* Vauréal Falls. With the river running low, it was a delicate curtain of lace drifting 250 feet or so through the air. Each droplet seemed to glisten briefly in the sunlight before vanishing in the cool pool below.

A certain philosopher, I've forgotten which one, observed that the characteristic movement of the human soul is in the form of a waterfall. As I gazed at this ethereal falls for—five minutes? twenty minutes? an hour? a year?—I agreed with the sentiment completely.

<hr />

You can't stay long on Anticosti without hearing about Louis-Olivier Gamache (1787–1854), the island's patron saint ... or patron devil. Known as The Wizard of Anticosti, he has been variously described as a *loup-garou* (werewolf), a bogeyman, a Satanist, and a pirate. Even today island mothers quiet their children with the threat: "Be good or Gamache will get you." The story goes that this shape-shifting, hard-living man died from drinking a beaker of clear rum before breakfast. Usually, he'd dilute his pre-breakfast rum with water. This time he didn't and paid the consequences.

Most stories about Gamache refer to his activities as a wrecker. They make him out to be the reason why so many shipwrecks have occurred here. He would light false beacons on the shore, and when a ship fetched up, he'd steal its cargo. In fact, Gamache wouldn't have needed to light a single beacon, for the island's shelving limestone shoals have the same effect on unsuspecting ships. More than three hundred wrecks rest in these waters, including several—the *Wilcox, Fayette Brown,* and *Calou*—still visible today, battered mementoes of nature's triumph on this most natural of islands.

Possibly Gamache was a model for the sailor-wrecker in Lever's *The Confessions of Con Cregan.* Another, more obvious model was the wreck of the brig *Granicus,* bound for Cork, Ireland, from Quebec City. In November 1829, a storm ran the *Granicus* aground at Fox Bay just in time for the severe Anticosti winter. Next spring a schooner from the Magdalen Islands put in at Fox Bay. In a newly-built house the schooner's crew found human carcasses strung from the ceiling. Over a fireplace hung two pots, one crammed with legs, the other with arms. There were also trunks full of human flesh, each piece seven by eight inches square and carefully salted. A dead man with a grossly distended belly lay in a hammock. He was a mulatto.

Having decided to visit the scene of this tragedy, I drove east across the island to Fox Bay, parked on a bluff, and then hiked down to a shingle beach, which I then followed for several miles. Even though it was quite foggy, I could still see the old dog-faces of grey seals peering at me from the water. On a nearby ledge cormorants were lined up like gentlemen at a black-tie ball. At last I reached Fox Bay, which consisted of a few rotting houses—dim, eerie presences in shrouds of fog. Since it was now raining and raining hard, I took refuge in one of these houses and had my lunch there.

Suddenly a woman appeared at the doorway. I gasped. As you too would gasp if you found out that you had company in a place as ghostly as Fox Bay. But the woman turned out not to be a ghost. She'd seen me in this cold house, on the cold floor, she said, and thought I might like to warm myself with a cup of coffee.

Lucille (for that was the woman's name) was one of the crew of a lobster boat that hailed from Sept-Îles on Quebec's north shore. They lobstered here in the summer and used as their base camp a makeshift hut directly across Fox River. She now took me to this hut in her motor launch. And when I walked in the door, the rest of the crew greeted me like a long-lost cousin. They hadn't seen a new face since they'd arrived here almost two months ago, so my new face was a source of delight to them. I was regaled with questions, slaps on the back, and food. Would you like a lobster, Monsieur? Some more coffee? Perhaps a freshly-caught salmon?

I asked them about the *Granicus*. Did any of them know where the cannibal feast had taken place?

"Why, Monsieur," Lucille declared, "it took place in the very house where you ate your lunch ..."

Two very different dining experiences under the same roof. I felt indeed fortunate to be among these good people, these good *well-fed* people, as a storm presumably similar to the one that grounded the *Granicus* began whipping at the windows of the little hut.

⟶•◆•⟶

I had one last thing to do on Anticosti. Years ago a large meteor supposedly fell somewhere on the island. A friend with astronomical leanings had asked me to photograph it, or at least to photograph the hole it'd carved in the ground. No one I talked to in Port-Menier knew about this meteor. But then an elderly woman mentioned a strange, crater-like pit near the Chaloupe River, maybe five miles off the road, maybe more, she wasn't certain of the exact location.

So I followed the Chaloupe for approximately five miles and then, compass in hand, began making westward forays into the bush. Happily, I wasn't assaulted by either mosquitoes or black flies (Menier's frogs had done a damn fine job). But each of my forays was repelled by the bush itself, an impenetrable mesh of old-growth spruce and forest tangle. As this was unexplored country, there were no paths, not even game trails. I almost tried, as per folkloric instruction, to walk on top of the trees.

Finally, I had to give up. My one consolation was a bag of bunchberries, a popular food item with northern Indians, especially the Montagnais, who mix them with fish grease.

Well, I did have another consolation—the knowledge that I'd left at least one stone, or meteor, unturned on Anticosti. Obviously, I'd have to return some day and continue my search.

NAPOLEON'S ISLAND

"What can be found so bare, so rugged all around? What so rude as to its inhabitants?" wrote the philosopher Seneca of Corsica, to which he'd been exiled for eight interminable years. During a recent, altogether more pleasant exile, I saw much of the island's bare and rugged scenery, but the only rudeness I encountered came from—myself. I'd made the mistake of ordering a simple *cuisine du pays* at a Calenzana restaurant situated just across from a church belfry that was full of hooting owls (Corsican owls seem to prefer churches to trees).

I hardly minded the owls, but the cuisine turned out to be a bit much. Literally, a bit much. I started with the *suppa corsa* (a hearty minestrone), then progressed to the *charcuterie* (a platter of meats, pig's brains, etc.) and *paté de grives* (thrush paté). Then came the *rifreda* (lamb roasted on a spit). Next was *lonzu* (smoked fillet of goat), with an ample side of haricote beans. As the *patron* advanced toward me with the cheese course in one hand, the fruit course in the other, I gestured despairingly. Enough! Now I knew why there were so many explosions in Corsica. Contrary to popular opinion, they didn't come from nationalists' bombs. They came from detonated diners ...

"Monsieur is perhaps sick?" asked the patron.

"Not sick, patron. Full."

"But Monsieur has yet to taste his very smelly, very Corsican cheese."

"*Tous mes regrets, patron.* One more bite and I'll burst." The patron gave me a stare that would have soured the milk of a good woman. I'd insulted his cuisine. Better to have insulted his manhood or his mother. For a moment I wondered whether he mightn't bring down an antique musket from the wall and use it to teach me a much-needed lesson in manners. Such lessons must be commonplace around here, I surmised. Else why would so many Corsican restaurants be equipped with arsenal decor?

Fortunately, this story has a happy ending. Instead of shooting me with an old fowling piece, the patron brought on the dessert course, a chocolate-cherry gâteau. I disposed of it willingly, even affectionately, and thus made a small but important step toward correcting my earlier gaffe.

⟫•⟪

As befits its most famous native son, Corsica is an island where the Napoleonic mood—at once epic and absurd, violent and gluttonous—sweeps aside most other moods. *Bamm!* A bomb blows up a foreign-owned vineyard. *Crash!* Another motor vehicle misses a hairpin curve on a tortuous mountain road and plunges ever downward to its doom.

Politically, Corsica is a *département* of France, but if you talk to a Corsican, it might seem the other way around. Why not? Over the centuries the Mediterranean trade winds have given this landfall so many invaders—Greeks, Arabs, Pisans, Genoese, Germans, even English—that its inhabitants can be forgiven for being just a little touchy, even chauvinistic about their identity. Maybe the son of an Ajaccio notary named Bonaparte can also be forgiven for his effort to redress some of history's wrongs at the expense of European geography.

But the Corsican mood does not always swallow up countries or cause road accidents. In search of an apéritif, one afternoon I stopped in at the Grande Hotel Napoleon Bonaparte in L'ile Rousse. I found this grand if slightly preposterous edifice (formerly the Palazzo Piccioni) irresistible, though I suspect the Emperor himself would have hated it. Here the Moroccan leader Mohammed V spent part of his exile, and to make him feel at home, a marble Bedouin tent was placed adjacent to the bar. In the billiard room, a jigsaw puzzle of Napoleon's coronation had been mounted lovingly on the wall, and in the lobby there was a four-sided clock each of whose sides told a different time. Among the guests a certain defunct gentility seemed to prevail. I would not have been at all surprised to see the Count of Monte Cristo shooting pool or the Pretender to the Austro-Hungarian throne enjoying a *pastis*. My own *pastis,* in fact, was on the house. Evidently the bartender must have mistaken my shabby journalistic self for shabby, deposed royalty.

This is an island where the indigenous language is so curious that it was once thought to be derived from Welsh-speaking American Indians. It's an island where southerners say that if Christ had been born in the north, He would have been a murderer, and the northerners say that if Christ had been born in the south, He would have been, horror of horrors, a Sard. It's an island of vendettas, evil eyes, and balcony lavatories. It has perhaps the highest density of high-performance cars in Europe, but nearly everybody you meet— a taxi driver, the roulette croupier at a village fête, even the man who runs the local pizzeria—is a shepherd. And why not? A Corsican shepherd can make upwards of $25,000 a year purveying his ewe's milk to the cheese industry in the mainland town of Roquefort.

The French consider Corsicans crude, ill-mannered, and backward, more or less the country bumpkins of the Mediterranean.

Corsicans return the compliment by pointing out that it used to be considered perfectly acceptable for a Frenchman to urinate in the stairways of the Louvre. Even so, there's no denying that Corsicans are a clannish, resolutely parochial people. They're more Italian than French, perhaps more Celtic than Italian. They build enormous mausoleums for their own deceased family members, but let the purported birthplace of Christopher Columbus lapse into a pile of glorified rubble. I suspect the Irish—another rubble-loving people—would have allowed Columbus's house to fall apart, too.

In fact, I mentioned the sorry state of Columbus's house to a resident of Calvi, where the house itself was located. Your people should be proud of it, I told him, or at least keep it in better condition, given Columbus's fame as an explorer. The man replied:

"Ah, that's the problem. Just the problem, Monsieur. We are still trying to figure out among ourselves whether the discovery of America is something we should be proud of ..."

———⇒•⇐———

To most people, if it doesn't call up images of bloody vendettas, the word Corsica calls up images of beaches. White or perhaps golden beaches, infinitely sandy, sunny, and sexy. Or maybe it evokes an azure Mediterranean whose warm waters caress the body like the sweetest, most gentle of masseuses. Alas, the truth is a little less cliché-ridden. In L'ile Rousse I couldn't even find the beach, though I knew it had to be somewhere beneath all that burnt flesh. And at Porto-Pollo, near Propriano, I bathed at a beach whose warm water turned out to be not significantly less mucky than Boston Harbor.

Yet the wise traveler need not despair. He can take a cue from the natives, for whom the seacoast always meant brute invaders rather than a good tan. These natives took to the mountainous interior of their island. So, I submit, should the traveler indifferent to sand. Take a walk in the Parc Naturel de la Corse (370,000 pristine acres). Pay a visit to the menhirs at Filitosa and Palaggiu. Inhale the salubrious alpine air at Vizzavona. And descend to the coast primarily to capture the rapturous pink and gold explosion of the Corsican sunset.

In my rented Renault, I took to the interior myself. I zigzagged north to south along a series of oleander-lined roads, following the green-stippled ridges that make up the island's backbone. I passed through one dizzily vertical village of grey granite and shuttered windows after another; and each village I passed through seemed sleepier than the last, as if they were all competing for the Brigadoon Prize.

Outside Aullene, an elderly woman dressed in black lifted her thumb at my approach. I'd seen many such women hovering on the sides of Corsican roads. They always maintain excellent eye contact with the approaching motorist, which they do, I'm convinced, to exploit the widespread fear of the evil eye. Refuse to pick them up and something not very nice may befall your expensive new car or, worse, your ungenerous person.

My old woman was going to Zonza. As I was driving the ancient Roman road to Solenzara, which passed through Zonza, I picked her up. She did not look like she possessed the evil eye. Cataracts, possibly, but not the evil eye. We conversed in bad French since that was the only French either of us knew. She told me that she thought Napoleon a nasty little man. Only people from Ajaccio, she said, had any interest in him. Occasionally they'd charter a boat and sail down to St. Helena to visit his death-place. The only thing she could think of that was sillier was their desire to put a Bonaparte back on the French throne.

At the end of the trip, the woman rewarded me with this piece of advice: If you go into a certain shop in Solenzara, Monsieur, wink at the proprietor and ask for some olive oil, you'll get a bottle of home-brewed myrtle liqueur that will—here I must intrude my own vernacular—knock your socks off. (Note: In Solenzara, I went into the shop and winked at the proprietor, whereupon he gave me a very strange look, along with some olive oil.)

Another day I parked my car and, like an old-time Corsican bandit, took to the maquis. That's the generic name for the spiky, aromatic shrub country in the island's outback. The maquis, it's said, pulled relentlessly at the exiled Napoleon's heart. This particular day it pulled not so much at my own heart as at my nose, for the curry-smelling immortelle plant was in abundant bloom. I felt like I was walking inside some sort of capacious Punjabi kitchen, albeit a Punjabi kitchen littered with granite boulders. After a while, I sat down for a rest and fell into a deep sleep. It was as if that masseuse I spoke of earlier had relocated her trade from the sea to this fragrant mound of earth, my bed.

———◆———

Corsica's statue-menhirs rise up from their carpets of maquis: megalithic warriors adrift in our own highly unmegalithic world. Swords forever at the ready, they may have been the island's first nationalists. Quite possibly they may also boast Europe's earliest portrait faces. Some of these faces are not wholly unlike the faces you see in the streets nowadays. Yet the identity of the craftspersons responsible for them—Torreans, archaeologists say, but *who* were the Torreans?—remains a mystery. Why the statues were erected—to "guard" religious sites?—remains something of a mystery, too. However, these venerable messieurs themselves seem rather to relish the mysterious aura which so completely surrounds their existence. You can see it in their almost whimsical grins.

Situated in the Taravo Valley, in the southeastern part of the island, Filitosa is Corsica's best-known megalithic site. To oblige its many visitors, Filitosa's menhirs have been propped up, rearranged, glued back together, even arrayed photogenically beneath a spreading olive tree. I must confess that I preferred the less domesticated site at Palaggiu, where the statues had been allowed to lean over, if they so desired, or even fall unceremoniously to the ground. That some of them were on the ground after standing up for so many centuries seemed to me only natural. Also, Palaggiu's menhirs—at least the ones more or less standing —still had a practical function: cattle, I observed, used them for rubbing-posts.

Yet it was at Filitosa, not Palaggiu, that I received a jolt of recognition. Walking among the menhirs, I happened to notice one whose squat face looked very familiar. Did I see in its ancient visage the old lady I picked up on the road? The patron who'd served me such terrifying portions of cuisine? The kindly barman at the Hotel Napoleon? I did not. Rather, I saw the squat-faced Napoleon himself. But it was a quite different Napoleon from last century's overachiever. This fellow seemed unusually content with his lot in life, as if it were far, far better to inhabit a piece of Corsican granite than to rule all of Europe.

❧

SCENES FROM THE
FORTUNATE ISLANDS

❧

Once upon a time, submarine upheavals off Africa's northwest coast created a scatter-pattern of seven lava chunks. Somewhat later, signs began to appear around the sandy verges of these lava chunks, now known as the Canary Islands. Signs that bore curious polyglot messages, such as *Man spricht deutsch* and *On parle français* and even *Watney's Red Barrel on Tap*. Still later appeared beach-front resorts and high-rise condos, ultra-chic clothing or no clothing at all, along with the ubiquitous Golden Arches of McDonald's.

VISIT THE SUNNY CANARIES proclaim travel posters, and sun-seeking Europeans arrive here by the millions. An Icelandic friend of mine, a sufferer of numerous bodily ailments, once told me that his chronic poor health had financed trips to the Canaries for at least half of his country's leading physicians.

Yet three of the islands—La Gomera, La Palma, and El Hierro— tend to be off the beaten track for even the most wide-ranging of Icelandic physicians. Indeed, they are so improbable of geography and scant of beaches that they remain more or less unvisited. Which is why, like Huck Finn lighting out for the Territory, I decided to visit them.

So it was that I flew to Tenerife and then immediately hopped the ferry for La Gomera. Behind me was a skyline of tourist hotels; ahead of me, twenty miles distant, rose a high grey-green bulk, seemingly impregnable. And right beside me at the rail, his gaze aimed homewards, was an elderly Gomeran. When at last our ferry arrived at the miniature capital of San Sebastián, this man tapped my shoulder lightly and pointed up, high up, to a formidable row of serrated massifs.

"There is La Gomera, Señor," he announced. The canal-map of his face creased into a beam of purest joy.

<hr>

Among other Canarios, Gomerans are considered a bit slow. There's even a La Gomera joke book which contains jokes about Gomerans similar to English jokes about the Irish or everyone's jokes about Poles: "Why can't you get cold milk in La Gomera?" "Because the Gomeran cannot fit his cow into the refrigerator." Or: "Why do Gomerans keep plenty of empty bottles around the house?" "For their friends who don't drink."

But it's hard not to be slow on an island which sits at a vertical tilt with the rest of existence. I was slow myself on La Gomera, and especially slow on its roads, which were so up-and-down that I wouldn't have traveled conspicuously slower had I rented a lethargic donkey instead of an automobile.

At this pace La Gomera felt like a continent rather than a 146-square-mile island. And as I drove along, I noticed what seemed to be bits and pieces borrowed from other continents, including an arid Saharan coast, Tuscan hill towns, Scottish highlands, a cloud forest, Caribbean banana plantations, and dizzying stone-banked terraces straight out of Bali.

Another thing I noticed about the island: even when it was inhabited, it appeared to be uninhabited.

Take Alojera. To get there, my guide Idilio and I crawled down a road whose tortuous zigzags resembled the lines on a seismograph. At the bottom of this road was Alojera itself—a dozen or so houses huddled together against a cliff like survivors in the stern of a lifeboat. The village seemed like an empty movie set; I saw no one there except a group of ancient women in fustian seated on a balcony and playing poker.

Also empty was Alojera's beach. A thunderous surf pounded against its black rocks with the eloquence of the Atlantic in its most vocal mood.

The road above Alojera was less empty, having been taken over by a shepherd and his flock. On the shepherd's shirt were printed these words: *Aquí partió Colón* (Columbus departed from here)— a reference to the fact that La Gomera was Columbus's final stop before his 1492 Atlantic crossing. That crossing must have been a piece of cake, I thought, compared to our own crossing of La Gomera.

"Ah," declared Idilio, pointing to the road. "Man walking his ghosts."

"Ghosts?" I said. "All I see are goats."

"Yes. Many ghosts. Gomerans eat ghosts, too ..."

I chuckled at this linguistic blunder. But the very next day I did find myself, if not among a flock of ghosts, at least in the suitably spectral *laurisilva* of Garajonay National Park.

This botanical relic of the Tertiary rests on a plateau which catches clouds pushed over the Canaries by the *alisio* (northeast trade winds). Whereupon these clouds unload their moisture as mist. The dense foliage retains this mist, so that it tends to be wet here even in years of drought. And not only wet, but on occasion—as I discovered—a little eerie, too.

I was walking alone in the Park, surrounded by swirls of mist. Laurels, Canary pines, evergreen myrtles, heather, old man's beard, tangles of vines, even blowdown—everything was cloaked in a kind of preternatural gauze. And except for the gentle soughing of the alisio, I didn't hear a single sound, not even a bird chirping. All at once I had an almost palpable sense of being watched. Watched by wary, forest-canny eyes.

It was in this same forest, I recalled, that the last of the island's Guanche aboriginals had hidden after the Spanish took over their homeland.

Suddenly I heard an odd scratching noise. It sounded as if someone was crawling over leaves and pine duff, crawling, in fact, towards me. The hairs went up on the back of my neck.

Then I located the source of the noise: a small lizard with an insect in its mouth. It was a perfect measure of the silence here that I could hear a lizard chewing on a fly.

<hr />

I encountered no Guanches, living or otherwise, among the laurel forests of Garajonay. For this blue-eyed, light-haired people—perhaps shipwrecked Vikings, perhaps a lost tribe of Israel, more probably the descendents of Berber emigrants from North Africa—had died out in La Gomera, as in all the other Canaries, a long time ago. By all accounts, they'd been an intriguing people: they mummified their dead in the Egyptian manner; they were cave-dwellers; they made baskets and pottery; they had no boats, large or small, and no interest in the sea; and they offered visitors refreshment of women's milk.

But had the Guanches really disappeared? One Sunday Idilio and I drove from San Sebastián to Chipude, a village rumored to possess the fairest skins and bluest eyes on the island. Chipudeans themselves were rumored to be ardent xenophobes who, a generation or two ago, greeted strangers by throwing stones at them; the Guanches hurled stones too, and with such accuracy that they drew admiration even from their Spanish targets.

But I encountered no such hostility in Chipude. Instead, a small boy grabbed my hand and offered to show me around, in return for which he only wanted a postcard from America, home of (he said glowingly) Daffy Duck. And a local restaurateur urged on me, with his compliments, a glass of *vino tinto* from his very own vineyard. That this wine tasted a bit volcanic did not matter; everything on this volcanic island, from grapes to goat cheese, from the goats themselves to dwarf potatoes called *papas arrugadas,* tastes volcanic.

We had chanced to arrive on the day when the Virgin of Candelaria, the village's patroness, was marched around the church square. This was quite an arresting sight: the richly-brocaded Virgin, borne aloft on a platform, towered weirdly above the procession. In front of her effigy danced several boys with a simple jigging motion of their bodies. One man, distinctly blonde-haired, was thumping on a goat-skin *tambour,* one-two-three THUMP, one-two-three THUMP, while another man clacked together a set of wooden *chácarones.* As for the Virgin herself, she swayed gently back and forth, as if she found the rhythm irresistible.

I suspect the Guanches might have done something similar with their sky-god Orahan, had the occasion arisen.

Later, on a nearby mountain-top, I heard what might have passed for an unearthly message from Orahan himself, although it was really just a conversation between two shepherds, Ramon and Isidro, both practitioners of *silbo.*

I'd situated these *silbadores* on adjoining mountain-tops, maybe a thousand feet from each other. To communicate would have required a cellular phone, which neither of them owned. But they had something better. Ramon stuck a knuckle in his mouth and produced a drawn-out fortissimo whistle, the meaning of which was: "The tax collector's coming!" Isidro's answer, also a whistle, came back: "Let's hide in the nearest cave!"

Legend has it that Gomeran Guanches once annoyed one of their chiefs so much that he cut off all their tongues; from then on, they could speak only through silbo. If this is true, it had at least one benefit, for a whistling language can span the island's up-and-down distances much better than speech.

Silbo, it's said, can be heard five miles away—imagine a thrush's song tweaked through a ghetto-blaster, and you'll get an idea of its volume. In fact, certain local songbirds have picked up silbo, which nowadays is more or less whistled Spanish, and now they sound like silbadores themselves.

I continued my experiment: "Ask Isidro to raise his left hand." Ramon whistled. Isidro instantly raised his left hand.

"And now tell him that you've decided to move to Spain, goats and all." Ramon produced a very long whistle, arching and falling in pitch, which inspired this whistled response:

"You must be *muy loco,* my friend. La Gomera is the best place in the world ..."

A sentiment that did not strike me, in the soft pearled hush of the island's twilight, as being altogether extreme.

La Palma is not to be confused with Las Palmas, capital of the Canaries, or with Palma, capital of Majorca, or in fact with Palm Springs, California. It is an island at once sensually rich and bleakly geologic, subtropical and snowed upon, deliciously aromatic and redolent of rotten eggs.

And it is an island of spiky, oozing, tentacled plants, or giants like *Echium pininana,* whose pale blue florets can grow to a height of thirteen feet. Many of these plants are endemic, a word that also describes La Palma itself.

As islands elsewhere are dominated by swathes of sand, soaring mountains, or turquoise lagoons, La Palma is dominated by a hole—

the vast horseshoe-shaped Caldera de Taburiente, a volcanic crater nearly six miles across, 19 miles in circumference, and with an inner wall that boasts an almost vertical drop of 2,300 feet. This giant among calderas was created thousands of years ago when erosive and tectonic forces brought about the collapse of several much smaller calderas.

Inside the Caldera, the only Guanches ever to put up any real resistance to Spanish rule once took refuge. But for a dirty trick, they might still be resisting even today. On May 3, 1493, the conquistador Alonso de Lugo tempted them out with an offer of peace; and as the trusting natives approached his camp, they were cut down by harquebus fire.

Yet, in a sense, they *are* resisting today. For although La Palma is governed by, in order of ascendancy, Tenerife, Gran Canaria, and Spain, it remains an island apart ... apart and maybe a little illusory, like a Ruritania of the Atlantic.

Here comes a van whose loudspeaker is so ragged-sounding that you can't tell whether it's announcing a funeral or selling fish. Here rests a full-scale cement model of Columbus's ship, the *Santa Maria,* with its nails lovingly painted on. Here, in this modern villa, lives a healer who'll cure you from the noxious effects of the evil eye by puffing cigar smoke in your face. Here lives a man, wholly Latin in complexion, who claims to be a direct descendant of Tanausu, the last Guanche chief.

And through it all, the entire island is singing. Bank tellers sing, waitresses sing, even women loading fodder on their donkeys sing, as if life were simply splendid here.

———>•<———

And yet it could all blow up at any moment. For not only is La Palma of volcanic origin, but it remains an emphatically active volcanic zone. Of this, *palmeros* themselves are quite proud. They'll compare their island to La Gomera, much to the latter's detriment, since poor, moribund Gomera hasn't blown up in years. They'll boast about an eruption of Tacande that cooked fish several miles out to sea. And they'll even inform you that Tenerife's El Teide (height: 12,200 feet) was created by their own Caldera (height: 7,950 feet) during one of its lesser upheavals.

One day I drove south from Santa Cruz, La Palma's capital, to the wine-producing village of Fuencaliente. Several miles from the village were two ominous-appearing cinder cones. The nearer cone, San Antonio, erupted in 1677 and buried the Holy Spring, Fuente Santa, from which Fuencaliente derives its name. When the other one, Teneguía, erupted on October 26, 1971, it enlarged the southern end of the island significantly; a local cigar, also called Teneguía, honors this occasion.

Teneguía is the island's most recent eruption. To reach it, I hiked through a Dantëesque landscape dotted with vineyards. Then I began climbing the cone's cindery slope.

The ground was still smoldering; various mephitic odors issued from its cracks. This is an excellent foretaste of Hell, I told myself, should I happen to end up there. I also thought about the seductive epithets once bestowed upon the Canaries; two of them, the Fortunate Islands (courtesy of Plutarch) and the Gardens of the Hesperides (courtesy of Herodotus), seemed especially inappropriate for the place where I was now walking.

There was a geodesic marker on the summit. And on this bare spike of metal, at least a mile from any consoling flush of greenery, I saw hundreds of crawling, climbing, frolicking, highly jubilant ladybugs. Had I chanced upon an entomological orgy? A gathering of the clans? An insectual power spot? I studied the ladybugs for several minutes. They were a reminder that even when La Palma looks most like a wasteland, it is still pulsing with life.

Later, back in Fuencaliente, I spoke with a local man who'd

witnessed Teneguía's eruption. He told me this:

"All the time I was looking at it, Señor, I was thinking one thing—what wonderful grapes will grow here when all of this is over ..."

⟶•◆•⟵

Literally celestial are the goings-on at the top of the Caldera de Taburiente, where an observatory, the Observatorio del Roque de Los Muchachos, rises in mystic detachment above the rest of the island. Centuries ago the Guanches reputedly flung unwanted children into the crater from these heights. Nowadays, however, the observatory's astronomers are engaged in a somewhat more congenial activity: the study of quasars, nebulae, and distant galaxies.

The summit of a volcanic caldera on a relatively remote island might seem an odd place for an observatory. Actually, it is an ideal place. For La Palma's remote skies are among the clearest in the whole world. And to uphold this clarity, a local edict, the so-called Law of the Sky, bans any type of light that might disturb astronomers at their nocturnal work.

One morning I set out to visit the observatory. The road was composed entirely of switchbacks; back and forth I drove, incessantly back and forth, through an ever-thinning forest of Canary pines. Also, this road—as if in emulation of a telescope—seemed to be trained on the sky. Thus I found myself driving up the Caldera at an almost vertical angle.

Every once in a while, a newly dislodged rock would tumble across the road in front of me, or directly behind me, and then continue its wayward course down the outer slope of the Caldera. One such rock was boulder-sized; it made me wonder whether I should have rented an armored car instead of a tinselly Toyota.

And then I was driving above the clouds. It was a strange sensation, as if my car had gone off the road and somehow gone into orbit. Off in the distance, also above the clouds, was the gleaming white pyramid of Tenerife's El Teide. But not only El Teide was white: when I reached the observatory, the ground was blanketed with snow. For a moment, I imagined myself in the subarctic rather than the subtropics.

The white observatory buildings blended in well with this white background. So did the telescope domes, which looked like grandiose igloos. Especially grandiose was the dome that covered the William Herschel Telescope, the third largest telescope in the world, named for an eighteenth-century German-English astronomer who believed each of the planets, including the sun, was inhabited by intelligent beings.

Whether the Herschel Telescope can locate an intelligent extraterrestrial being, or even an unintelligent one, remains to be seen. But it can spot an ant on the coast of Africa two hundred miles away.

In the observatory's Residencia, I met a Dutch astronomer named Henrik who informed me that the Herschel Telescope costs $15,000 a night to run—and is four times oversubscribed; that its precision rivals the Hubble Space Telescope; that last night it logged fifteen new "objects," among them a new quasar; that much of the current work at the observatory centers around the study of brown dwarfs; and that La Palma's only drawback as an astronomical viewing site was the occasional sandstorm blowing in from the Sahara.

After lunch, I left the Residencia and walked to the rim of the Caldera. Some of the snow had already melted, exposing a few scraggly alpine plants, along with stabs of volcanic red, orange, and yellow on the surrounding rocks.

Soon I found a trail that led to the highest point on La Palma, the Roque de los Muchachos. The eponymous *muchachos* are columns of dark red solidified mud which supposedly look like little boys at play. If so, they look like badly eroded little boys at play. To me, they seemed much more like the ruins of some long-abandoned castle, complete with fantastic turrets, bastions, and wasted walls.

Immediately below me was the Caldera's crater, with its precipitous slopes and flying buttress ridges rising from a sea of clouds. Somewhere down there, in depths of rock, was the lush rift valley where the resistant Guanches had lived. Down there too was the sacred Guanche monolith Idafe, a finger pointed accusingly towards the heavens. But all I could see were billowy, fleecy clouds.

Above me, the wide vault of the sky stretched out to the distant horizon. It was a sky clearer, more exultantly blue than any sky I'd ever seen. Likewise it seemed so close that I felt I could reach up and touch it, perhaps give it a nudge of approval. For it was a perfect sky; perfect for astronomers and non-astronomers alike.

<hr/>

From La Palma I flew southwest to El Hierro, the smallest and most isolated of all the Canaries, an island which once was considered the literal end of the world but now has fallen off the world's map. And in falling off, it seems to have landed in an attitude of perpetual slumber. This was an attitude picked up by the locals. "Time for a siesta," one of my guides would announce every hour or two, then fall instantly, blissfully asleep. But I've seldom slept so well myself as I slept on this most tranquil of islands.

There was nothing sleepy, however, about the island's dogs. Or at least about one of its dogs. One morning I was strolling past what appeared to be a derelict house a mile or so from my hotel when a big Canarian mastiff—a brindled, smooth-haired, vaguely jackal-like creature—came charging out and sank its broad jaws firmly into my haunch.

It was a painful moment; revenge, I figured, for the dogs I'd eaten over the years in Greenland and the Pacific. It was also a none-too-subtle reminder that the Canaries probably owe their name to this venerable breed of canine (the word Canary comes from the Latin *canis*) and not, perish the thought, little yellow-bellied birds.

But whatever its mode, biting or non-biting, slumberous or awake, El Hierro never failed to surprise me. One evening a local restaurateur offered me a glass of *parra,* a raw spirit distilled from the lees of wine-making and similar to the French *marc* or the Italian *grappa.* Then he brought out, just for my benefit, a large, slightly weathered box of corn flakes, along with a bowl of milk. For he'd heard somewhere that Americans subsist almost entirely on corn flakes. And he would not allow me to go without my subsistence cuisine, not on *his* island.

———⇒•⇐———

Like La Palma and La Gomera, El Hierro is Spanish, but only just. I often felt that it was like Ireland in that country's misty, melancholy mood. It had endless traceries of dry stone walls, many of them collapsed. Wherever I looked, there seemed to be ruined stone houses, usually shrouded by fog. And everywhere, too, there was a sense of people having pulled up their stakes and gone off to more lucrative, although not necessarily better shores.

Sometimes, even in the middle of the day, the only sound on El Hierro seemed to be the distant guttural of a donkey or the tintinnabulation of goat bells. At such times I'd feel the island's emptiness almost as a physical presence.

At other times I'd notice an untended fig-tree and recall how, not so long ago, a tree like this would have been considered such a prized possession that a paterfamilias would bequeath each of its branches to a different offspring. Now it was simply contributing to the general dereliction.

Still, El Hierro's images stayed in my mind. I'd see a shepherd striding out of the mists, a visitant in a cape and a wide-brimmed Rubens hat. Or I'd see a group of old men fiercely clattering dominoes in a bar. Once I even saw a figure vaulting down the steep cliffs of El Risco with a long pole called an *asta*. This wasn't a dotty stunt like bungee-jumping. For astas are (or were) the local version of the alpenstock; their use dates back to Guanche times.

But it was on the remote windswept slopes of El Julan that I found perhaps the most haunting of the island's images—the prehistoric site of Los Letreros.

Actually, I couldn't find the site at first and ended up bushwhacking all over the slope. With each step, I collected dozens of tiny, velcro-like *amor seco* ("dry love") petals on my socks. Once, pausing to remove them, I took the opportunity to munch on some corn flakes—a trail food I now possessed in quantity. And as I munched, I saw a dead sheep only a few feet away, its intestines flowering in the sunlight.

At last I came upon Los Letreros. The site turned out to be an astonishing array of inscriptions, squiggles, wiggles, doodles, whirligigs, digits, circles, and wheels carved into a lava-stream. It was so large that I spent well over an hour just walking around it. And having walked around it, I had to confess that I was no less stumped than the experts.

For no one knows quite what to make of these inscriptions. Do they represent the letters of some long-lost alphabet? Or might they be some sort of ancient graffiti? Were they carved over a long period of time, thousands of years maybe, or in a relatively short time? And what vanished race carved them? Probably not the Guanches, since they don't look much like the Guanche petroglyphs found elsewhere in the Canaries. They look more like the drawings of children ... or the mad.

There was a uncanny beauty about Los Letreros. It hardly bothered me that the site's meaning might be lost to the ages. Indeed, I felt a certain frisson of pleasure at being in the presence of a perhaps insoluble mystery.

<hr/>

My last day on El Hierro I went to the end of the world.

This is not just a metaphor. Intersected by Ptolemy's ancient meridian line, El Hierro was once regarded as the most westerly landfall in the known world; beyond the island's own most westerly point, Punta Orchilla, a traveler ran the risk of being swallowed up either by sea monsters or oblivion. In fact, Punta Orchilla stood exactly on the prime meridian until the end of the eighteenth century.

From the Faro de Orchilla I hiked with my guide Antonio to the old meridian marker at Punta Orchilla. It was a hot, sun-baked day; a day made even hotter by the fact that the lava on which we were walking absorbed the heat and then flung it back at us in great blistering waves.

This lava itself was a geometry of shapes so gnarled and contorted that they looked like the victims of some terrible inner torture. Much of it was covered by the bright orange orchil lichen from which Punta Orchilla takes its name. Here and there, in a bubble cave or crevasse, I noticed the bones of sheep and goats. I also noticed middens of limpet shells, evidence of a Guanche presence even at the end of the world.

And Punta Orchilla did seem like, if not the actual end of the world, at least a hot, gargoylish, bone-littered facsimile thereof.

After forty-five minutes, we reached the meridian's grey cement marker. I was just getting ready to relax in its cool shade when Antonio suddenly pointed out to sea and exclaimed:

"Look! San Borondón's Isle!"

Then, as my eyes scanned the horizon, he admitted that he was having a little joke at my expense. For San Borondón's Isle, which reputedly lies five degrees west of El Hierro, may or may not exist. Both Ptolemy and Pliny mention it. It is on the maps used by Columbus and on the celebrated globe of Martin Behaim. In 1519, it was formally included in the Canary group as the "Unfound Island." Four times between 1526 and 1721 the Spanish mounted expeditions to search for it. One expedition even brought along a full complement of priests to exorcise the island's doubtless evil spirits; but San Borondón, even at the bidding of the Church of Rome, refused to appear.

And now it had refused to appear for me, too.

But I was hardly disappointed by this. For I'd already seen three islands no less fanciful than this fly-away isle—three strange, beguiling, elusive islands that were unfound themselves, gloriously so.

LAWRENCE MILLMAN

RENDEZVOUS
WITH A GIANT

I have a confession to make: I've never jogged with Bill Clinton, dined with Robert Redford, or danced with Madonna. In fact, I can claim no brush whatsoever with celebrity—unless you count the time I shared a piece of half-rotten seal meat with East Greenland's last heathen. But I have met a giant; a giant neither of this world or the next, but of the far away pelagic world that borders on myth. And this meeting is etched so clearly into my mind that it could have happened yesterday, although it happened on February 4, 1980.

The place was Plum Island, a seven-mile-long sliver of sand and dune, scrub and marsh joined to Newburyport, Massachusetts, by a bridge. I was walking with my friend Betty along a section of the island's Atlantic-fronting beach. It was an exceptionally cold day even for February. A blustery wind off the sea made the already subzero temperature seem like thirty or forty below. As a sometime arctic wanderer, I found this exhilarating. But Betty, who preferred palm trees to permafrost, did not.

"My body is starting to feel hypothermic," she told me, "and that's only the warm part ..."

"All right," I said. "We'll walk as far as that old wreck up ahead.

Then we'll turn back."

But as we got closer to this wreck, it began to look less like a wreck and more like a beached whale. Then as we got still closer to it, I could see that it wasn't a beached whale. For what beached whale is bulbous at one end, tapered at the other, and pink in color? What beached whale has long snakelike arms, a huge beak, and eyes like pie plates?

"Good Lord!" exclaimed Betty. "What is it?"

"Good Lord!" I said, scarcely aware that I was echoing her. "It's … it's … a giant squid!"

I was flabbergasted. Blown away. Knocked for a loop. Rendered speechless. These aren't very literary expressions, I know, but they describe exactly how I felt as I stood next to the creature's enormous body. I stared at its parrotlike beak, which was locked into a seemingly defiant skyward gape, as if the squid had died trying to devour the sun.

But was it indeed dead? In order to be certain, I gave it a nudge or two with my foot. And when it didn't respond, I lay down in the cold sand to get its measurements. The mantle was two feet longer than I was, which made it eight feet long. I unfurled one of the arms and found that it was a little less, perhaps seven feet long. Further along the beach I discovered a tentacle that had been partially gnawed by a dog, a dogfish, or an inordinately hungry beachcomber. It was approximately fifteen feet long. Which meant that this monarch of the continental shelf, when intact, would have been almost thirty feet in length. Thirty feet! No wonder such creatures can wrestle sperm whales.

"You know, I've completely forgotten about the cold," Betty said. Even so, she kept her distance from the squid, as if she expected one of its arms suddenly to wriggle up and grab her. Seeing her fear, I remembered my own childhood fear of the villainous giant squid in *Twenty Thousand Leagues Under the Sea*. And it seemed to me that if a creature like the one lying in front of us did not exist, only a writer with Jules Verne's imperial imagination could have invented it.

I'd read enough about giant squids to know how rare they are. So we hurried to the car and drove to the island's coast guard station. The man behind the desk shook his head when he heard my breathless account of our discovery.

"Squids aren't really in our jurisdiction," he said. "Now if you had seen a sinking ship ..."

Undaunted, I found a pay phone and rang up the New England Aquarium, whose curator, John Prescott, was an acquaintance of mine. John was no less flabbergasted than Betty and I. The next day he sent up a refrigerator truck from Boston, along with several muscular aquarium employees to hoist the squid—which weighed 450 pounds—off the beach.

Our discovery turned out to be even rarer than I thought. Only a hundred or so giant squids had washed ashore worldwide in the last century. And none had fetched up on the east coast of North America since 1908. This gave our squid a certain cachet with the media. Several New England newspapers featured it in stories, one of which boasted this headline: *Incredible Calamari Found on Plum Island*. Not to be outdone, a TV newsman peppered his story with references to King Kong and Godzilla.

Some time later, I decided to visit my squid in its new home, so I drove down to the Aquarium from where I was living in Maine.

"Ah," said the ticket-taker, "*you're* the guy that found the monster." Then she directed me to a hermetically sealed, glass-topped case.

Since I'd last seen it, the squid looked much the worse for wear, as if dozens of eager hands had prodded, probed, and pummeled it in an effort to learn its secrets. Not only that, but it looked curiously sad. And maybe it was sad, too—sad at being plucked from its not-quite-final resting place on a tranquil North Atlantic beach. Or perhaps I was merely registering my own sadness at the sight of this much-diminished version of a giant I once knew.

Eighteen years later I still make the occasional visit to Plum Island. If I'm alone, I'll walk around the marshes with my binoculars, searching for bald eagles and snowy owls. But if I happen to be with someone, more than likely I'll take a stroll down the beach to a place I always seem to recognize, although it doesn't have any obvious features. Then I'll point down to the sand and tell a story about a deep-sea creature cast up on these alien shores, cast up broken yet somehow whole.

LAWRENCE MILLMAN

IN THE BACK
OF BEYOND

GETTING MY GOAT

Candelaria, Ecuador, is thirty-five miles southeast of the popular watering hole of Baños, at the end of a tortuous, looping track. There are only two reasons to include it on your itinerary: (1) If you happen to be a Peace Corps volunteer looking for work. (2) If you're climbing L'Altara, the 18,000-footer that lies directly behind the village. I'd come for the latter reason—to test my limbs against the steepdown pinnacle of L'Altara.

Yet before testing those limbs, I needed to fuel them. I stopped an Indian bent under a bundle of faggots and asked him where I could grab a bite to eat. For every Andean hamlet, no matter how dingy, has some sort of restaurant. The Indian pointed a finger toward a low-slung, mud-and-wattle dwelling with a dead dog a few feet from its front door.

The place did not inspire confidence. But since I wasn't exactly looking for haute cuisine, I figured I could take whatever local specialty the restaurant dished up. So I walked over, stooped, and entered what turned out to be a musty room lit by a single flickering candle. There was only one item of furniture—a semi-collapsed bench on which sat an old *campusino* drinking from a bottle of hooch. At the other end of the bench an enormous cockroach was drinking from a syrupy puddle. I sat down between them.

A slight, dark-hued man was staring at me. "I'd like something to eat, Señor," I told him.

The man smiled. "Antonio," he said, shaking my hand.

"Larry."

"You are perhaps climbing L'Altara, Señor Larry?"

"I am. Tomorrow."

Antonio told me about Hermann, a Swiss climber who fell off L'Altara last month and got battered on the rocks below. "Dead?" I asked. "Dead as mutton," he smiled.

Funny he should have used that phrase. A bit ominous, too. It was mutton that I planned to ask him for, thinking it the most readily available meat in these parts. Immediately, I switched to goat.

"You shall have it." He shouted *Manuel!*, and a boy emerged from one of the back rooms. He gave the boy a few sucres. "My son will get *chivo* from the village. Meanwhile, you would perhaps care for a drink?"

"Yes," I said. "*Malta*." Malta was a dark beer with the proverbial egg mixed into it.

"I have no malta."

"*Naranjilla,* then." This is an Ecuadorian fruit juice that has the not unpleasant flavor of bitter orange.

"I have only *agua*."

"Well, agua it is. Bottled."

"You shall have it." He brought out a large transparent flask that bore only the slightest resemblance to a bottle. Its so-called water was slate-grey in color and doubtless harbored an army of amoebas poised for attack.

"On second thought," I said, "I'll pass on the agua."

Now I settled back on the bench. Soon I noticed an incredibly wizened crone hunched up on the dirt floor and staring at me.

"That is my mother, Señor Larry," Antonio said. "And the person sitting next to you, he is my father." (This guy runs a family restaurant, I thought, or maybe he's just running a family.)

Half an hour passed. I tried to study my topo map of L'Altara, but there wasn't enough light to make out a single contour, much less the lay of the mountain itself. On the other hand, there was quite enough light for my host's clutch of offspring, stationed at every doorway, to study me. Four boys, three girls, and several unclassified infants, all staring with the abnormally large eyes of Mexican children painted on velvet.

"You don't see many gringos around here, do you?" I said to Antonio.

"Very few. The last was Señor Hermann. He was battered on the rocks."

"Dead as mutton."

"You have it."

An hour passed. No Manuel, no chivo. I was beginning to think this a not very satisfactory dining experience. It was fine, of course, if you liked being stared at. Otherwise, it suggested famine and drought, with a dash of pestilence thrown in as well.

"Señor Antonio," I said, "your son has been gone for well over an hour. Why is he taking so long?"

"He must take long. For you, Señor Larry, are an honored guest and he must find you the very best chivo in the village. That's what the boy is doing now. Bargaining for your chivo."

"How much longer will he be bargaining for my chivo?"

"Not more than two hours ..."

Two more hours of this and I'd be a slavering idiot. Not only a slavering, but a pretty damned peeved idiot, too. So I implored Antonio to feed me some food, *any* food, while we were waiting for Manuel. He seemed to ponder this request, mentioned a *sopa de maíz,* but then went on to say that it really wasn't good enough for an honored guest like me.

"It'll be good enough, I assure you."

Within fifteen minutes Antonio had brought out a bowl, which I quickly lifted to my lips, only to discover that he'd been right: the soup wasn't good enough for me. It tasted like postage stamp glue. This, in itself, was not surprising, since postage stamps are gummed with corn and cassava, two items always present in sopa de maíz. The soup tasted worse than postage stamp glue. What's more, it had enough salt in it to clog the arteries of a blue whale. I exploded:

"What kind of restaurant is this? First you can't locate a goat in a land overrun with goats. Then you serve me this soup. No wonder you don't have any customers here ..."

"Restaurant?" said Antonio. "But this isn't a restaurant, Señor Larry. It is my own home."

"Your ... home?"

"Of course. If you want a restaurant, there is a small one next door."

I felt lower than the lowest mite on a llama's backside. To think: I'd mistaken this poor man's abode for an eatery, making uncivil demands on him even as he was doing his best to treat me like a visiting dignitary. I muttered a few hopelessly inadequate words of apology. Then (God help me!) I lifted the bowl once again to my lips. And God must have indeed helped me, for the sopa de maíz began to taste, if not actually good, at least more palatable. I nodded my approval.

"Taste good?" Antonio said.

"Like heaven," I replied.

A short while later Manuel returned from his quest for the ultimate goat. Apparently his father had given him only enough sucres for a very ordinary goat, so he'd come back, sad to say, empty-handed. I tried to give him a few more sucres for his trouble, but Antonio brushed away my hand, saying:

"Oh no. It's been our pleasure, *amigo*."

"On the contrary," I told him, "it's been *my* pleasure."

So ends a cautionary tale of dining out in the High Andes. Well, not quite. I still had to mount an exit that would not hurt anybody's feelings. Smiling and shaking hands all around, I performed this task with some success, but then as I stepped from the house, I tripped over the dog. The poor animal let out an alarmed yelp and went running down the road. It wasn't dead, after all.

THE LOST
REPUBLIC

Up goes the steep footpath from New Hampshire's Route 3. As I climb, I see a moose skull protruding from an embankment like an early Pleistocene relic. I pass under a couple of old-growth spruce rendered dwarflike by the elements. Now I find a bolus of scat which my companion, Gordon Coville, identifies as belonging to a pine marten. And now I pause to inhale the fragrant scent of balsam fir; a scent so invigorating that it nearly lifts me off my feet.

Gordon, a retired logging inspector for Champion Lumber, seems to be on intimate terms with every tree, stump, and piece of blowdown within a twenty-five mile radius. All his stories seem to connect with trees, too. He says his grandfather was taught how to read and write by an old Abenaki Indian named Archie Annance. Not having any paper, Archie used a perfectly appropriate writing material for these parts—birch bark.

At last we arrive at a stagnant beaver pond half a mile from the Canadian border. There's not a more unlikely destination in all of New England than this two-acre pond, known as Fourth Connecticut Lake. Its surface is covered with moss-rafts. Old bleached stumps angle out of it like huge crooked fingers. No fish inhabit its needle-strewn, acidic shallows. There aren't any beavers around, either.

We step through the marsh grass to the pond's southern edge. Now Gordon gestures to a little silvery rill. "There it is," he says. "The headwaters of the Connecticut River ..."

This rill trickles down to the much larger Third Connecticut Lake, from which it will gather momentum before pouring into Second and First Connecticut Lakes. Soon it will become the mighty river which separates New Hampshire from Vermont. Then it will flow through the farmlands of central Massachusetts and past the glassed-in insurance offices of Hartford, Connecticut. And then, exactly 407 miles from where we're standing, the Connecticut River will spill over shallow sandbars and into Long Island Sound.

Suddenly I have an anarchistic thought: What would happen if I tossed a log or two over this little rill? Would New England dry up?

———◦•◦———

The Connecticut Lakes country is the very tip of the geographical finger New Hampshire extends northward. "Northward" is perhaps the operative word here. The region's average mean temperature is 37°F; Boston, by contrast, is the malarial tropics. Twice during my late September visit, cold fronts swept down from Labrador and made me feel as if I were actually in Labrador.

This is New England's back of beyond. It has no tastefully reconstructed historical districts, no clapboard taverns promoting the letter "e" (as in "Ye Olde Groggerie"), and no shops purveying genteel outdoorwear. To get here, you can't take the wrong road amid the cancerous growth of North Conway and somehow expect to pull up at First Connecticut Lake. You must take a number of wrong roads, all increasingly less trafficked, and even then you'll probably end up south of here, in Lancaster or Dixville Notch. That's because north country roads tend to be all over the map, splendidly gnarled and meandering. In an era of straightlining, they defer to the natural contours of the land and the switchbacks of rivers and streams rather than human artifice.

Only when you leave Colebrook ("We left Colebrook and civilization," Francis Parkman wrote in his 1841 travel journal) and begin climbing the roller-coaster of Route 145 will you be on the right road. After a few miles, you'll pass a historical marker commemorating the life of a local Cooashuake Indian, Metallak, who died in 1847 at the age of one hundred and twenty. It's said that Metallak knew the wilderness so well that he guided people through it even after he went blind. And if that seems extraordinary, well, this happens to be extraordinary country.

It is also country very much apart. Where else in New England can you still stumble upon tracts of old-growth forest? What other part of New Hampshire can't pick up New Hampshire TV and radio stations? Where else is white pine referred to as "punkin pie" on account of its golden color and fine grain? And where else is the main problem among teenagers not drugs or booze but broken snowmobiles?

In the last century, much of it was quite literally apart, too. The story goes like this:

Both the United States and Canada claimed the 250 square miles between Hall's Stream and Indian Stream. As a result, both countries taxed a citizenry who were not especially eager to pay taxes to one country, much less two. On July 9, 1832 (the Glorious Ninth?), these citizens held a town meeting in which, by an overwhelming vote of 56 to 3, they declared themselves a separate nation, the Republic of Indian Stream.

This upstart nation was a curious blend of old-fashioned democracy and the Marx Brothers. All work was performed on a voluntary basis. The payment of debts was strictly a matter of honor. The jail was a 700-pound inverted potash kettle set on a rock next to Sheriff Reuben Sawyer's house. The General Assembly and the voting population were one and the same. And in the event of an attack by a foreign power, everyone had an arsenal of rocks to fling at the intruders (muskets were too expensive).

The Indian Stream Republic survived as a sovereign entity for three not very happy years. Crime was so endemic that even the jail was stolen. Demon rum was worshipped to such a degree that it threatened to dislodge God as a religious entity. A group of Indian Streamers who wanted to annex Canada drunkenly abducted a Canadian sheriff, nearly provoking an international incident. Finally, the New Hampshire militia marched in and took over the republic. Thus ended one of our country's more unusual experiments in self-government.

Nothing is left today of this lost republic, no Liberty Bell, Independence Hall, or "rude bridge." Nothing, that is, except a word old-timers occasionally use in reference to their granitic home: they call it the Republic.

———❖———

Tourism hasn't corroded deeply here. Those few tourists who do turn up tend to be mostly outdoorsy types, people with mud permanently caked on their shoes, a mangy dog or two in attendance, and binoculars at the ready. Often you see them with a cup of coffee in Baldwin's General Store in Pittsburg, the region's only town. That this coffee doesn't come from beans harvested in Kenya or the New Guinea highlands hardly seems to bother them.

The region's chief (or at least most obvious) attraction is, strange to tell, its moose wallows. One wallow in particular always seemed to have at least half a dozen moose, as well as half a dozen moose watchers, whenever I drove past it. The moose observed such regular hours that I wondered if they were on the payroll of the state's Department of Tourism.

Viewing these roadside moose seemed to me somewhat like

viewing animals in a zoo. Nice, but a bit *too* nice. So one day I drove off to find moose in a wilder setting. I followed a dusty, winding logging road for fifteen or so miles, past Mt. Magalloway, until I came to a small pond that didn't even rate a mention on my topo map. It was a clone of Fourth Connecticut Lake—shallow, murky, and littered with debris.

An ideal spot for moose, I thought, and parked my car.

I found a strip of birch bark and rolled it into the shape of a megaphone. Then I put my mouth to the opening and called out in a rising voice, *oouwwaaa, oouwwaaa*. This attempt at a moose call was considerably easier on my resources than trying to imitate the sound of a cow moose urinating.

I waited. A red squirrel scolded me for disturbing his afternoon siesta, but that was it. No moose appeared.

I called out again. Again, no moose. So I settled down with *Spiked Boots,* Robert Pike's book of north country vignettes. Every once in a while, I'd look up in case a moose had belatedly responded to my call. I read about Ginseng Willard, who, having killed over a thousand porcupines, made a necklace from their claws. I also read about how Metallak salted his dead wife in the winter in order to bury her more or less intact in the spring. I was just getting to the section on the Indian Stream Republic when I heard what sounded like a large boat being launched.

A large boat in this secluded place? I got ready to be annoyed, but then I saw a bull moose splashing into the water in search of aquatic browse. I put down my book very quietly. Not quietly enough, though, because suddenly the moose looked up (moose reputedly use their antlers like satellite dishes, to attract sound), noticed me, and then splashed out of the water and into the woods. The last I saw of him was the glint of his giant antlers against the crisp autumn sky.

On the way back, I got lost and drove around for an hour on a series of logging roads, none of which, I'm pleased to say, could have accommodated a high-performance vehicle. They hardly accommodated my own low-performance vehicle. At last I came out near a moose wallow just off New Hampshire's Route 3. There were perhaps ten people looking at what must have been a singularly self-conscious moose.

Poor thing, I thought. Better to be a fleeting, glinting vision, like my moose, than a magnet for voyeurism.

———※◦※———

The following day I rented a rowboat and rowed out into the middle of First Connecticut Lake. Then I set down my oars and just stared out at the water. The *undeveloped* water. The Connecticut Lakes are maintained as reservoirs by New England Power, which means there aren't any speedboats cutting obscene swathes across them or resort facilities squatting anywhere on their shores.

I sat in my boat and tried to imagine the winter day in 1900 when the last herd of caribou in New England walked across the ice of this very lake and clambered out on the other side. Whether they ended up in Canada or just died out no one seems to know, for they were never seen again—eleven or twelve animals en route to oblivion.

Lost in reverie, I hadn't noticed that it had begun to rain. Then one particularly robust raindrop whacked me on the head, and I did notice it. Moments earlier I'd been able to make out shoreline birches as individual showers of gold. Now all I could see was a general blurriness. Not having brought along any raingear, I pulled for the nearest stretch of shore. Once I got there, however, the rain stopped just as abruptly as it'd started. A phenomenon known to anyone who has ever put a boat in the water.

But since I was already ashore, I decided to do a little exploring. I bushwhacked through a canopy of trees that probably hadn't seen an axe in a hundred years. Then I crossed a couple of snow-mobile trails, one of which I followed to a clearing. Here I found a dilapidated cabin, its door clawed repeatedly by spring-hungry bears. From the window I peered in and saw an old camp bed standing upright against the wall. A kerosene lamp, glass broken, lay on the table.

On this same table was a faded note. I squinted, craned my neck, and then squinted some more, but all I could read were a few words: "... in the lap of Nature ... wish you were here, too ... I chopped some wood for you ... logs out back." Someone seemed to have borrowed this cabin God knows when, from God knows whom, and had long since vacated the premises. I walked around to the back, but the logs referred to in the note were long gone themselves, either burned in the cabin's stove or crumbled away.

Now I returned to my boat. As I was untying it, I heard a loud tremulous wail sweep across the lake. It was a genuinely eerie sound, at once maniacal and not quite of this world. I wondered: Has the cabin's guardian spirit, displeased with my visit, pursued me here? Or could it be old Metallak himself raising a war cry from the Land of the Dead?

Then I saw a loon—symbolic bird of the North—floating low in the water, only its head and neck visible. It dove down for a fish, came up again, and again roused the lake with its cry. A cry which now seemed to me like a benediction.

I watched and listened as a scarlet sunset fired the sky just beyond the sharp-pointed treetops on the other side of the lake.

Then I began pulling for home.

OUR MAN
IN EVEREST

If Maurice Wilson had not existed, it's highly unlikely that a member of the scribbling trade would have thought to invent him. Instead, we'd beseech our Muses to come up with someone a bit less outrageous, like, for example, Sir Edmund Hillary. But Maurice Wilson did exist, strange to say. And even stranger to say, he continues to exist, a testimony, of sorts, to the human spirit.

Born in Bradford, Yorkshire, in 1898, the son of a well-to-do woolens manufacturer, Maurice seemed headed for the same kind of stolid career as Wilson *père* when the Great War intervened. The young man fought at Ypres, after which he suffered fatigue, depression, inexplicable aches and pains. No doctor could help him, so he turned to a homeopath, a man with decidedly Eastern whims.

Food's the problem, always is, this doctor informed Maurice. Food's bad for a person's body. Just fast for a couple of weeks, old chap, and you'll be as good as new.

Maurice had nothing to lose, so he subsisted for thirty-five days on a diet of rice-water, with a few slugs of meditation thrown in. By the thirty-fifth day he indeed seemed to be, if not as good as new, at least better than he'd felt in a long, long time. Shortly thereafter he had a vision in which an unusually thin but otherwise robust God appeared to him. The Supreme Being seemed to be taking the cure, too.

From then on Maurice set himself the task of bringing this cure before the eyes of the world. One day he happened on a newspaper cutting about the ill-fated 1924 Everest Expedition. He read it through with interest, deciding that if mountaineers Mallory and Irvine had only fasted, they would have reached the hitherto unreachable summit of Everest, lived to tell the tale, and likewise been able to forgo the hateful task of high-altitude cookery. To prove his point, he concocted a plan for his own personal Everest expedition. He would fly solo to the mountain, crash his plane on East Rongbuk Glacier, and—dosing himself with rice-water—trot up to the summit, Union Jack patriotically in hand.

There were just two practical objections to Maurice's plan. He knew nothing about mountain climbing and he couldn't fly a plane. Mere details. He bought a secondhand Gipsy Moth, rechristened it *Ever Wrest,* and proceeded to take flying lessons at the London Aero Club. That he earned his pilot's license is indicative of the loose if not downright unfettered standards of the time. As for climbing, he made a few modest scrambles in Snowdonia and pronounced himself fit. The prospect of altitude sickness didn't trouble him. For he reasoned that the less food his body took in, the more room it'd have for oxygen, a commodity he knew to be rather more scarce on Everest than in North Wales.

By April 1933 he was ready to gatecrash the mountain Tibetans call Chomolungma, the Mother Goddess of the Earth. But first he decided to say goodbye to his parents. En route to Bradford his engine cut out and he crashed into a farmer's hedgerow. He was unhurt. Undaunted, too. A month later, he was ready to try again. But now the Air Ministry caught wind of his eccentric plan and sent him a restraining order in the form of a telegram. He tore up this telegram and off he flew. Somehow *Ever Wrest* managed to sputter and wheeze a passage as far as Darjeeling, India, but there it was impounded. Well, I'll just have to walk the rest of the distance, Maurice announced. The British refused him permission to enter Tibet on foot, too. So he simply disguised himself as a Sherpa and, as promised, walked the rest of the distance.

On April 12, 1934, Maurice reached Rongbuk Monastery. Two days later he set off by himself to ascend the Mother Goddess of the Earth. His most important item of gear was a shaving mirror. This he intended to use as a heliograph from the summit, so the world would know of his success. With an ice-axe borrowed from the head lama, he began hacking steps, none of which led in the direction of the summit. At one point he found some discarded crampons, but such was his ignorance—nay, innocence—that he just threw them away, having no idea what they were for. His haphazard ascent was finally brought to a halt by whiteout conditions. In his diary he wrote: "No use going any further ... It's the weather that has beaten me—what damned bad luck!"

Back at the monastery he engaged the services of two local Sherpas, Rinzing and Tewang, for another assault on the mountain. They'd show him the proper route to the summit, he reasoned, and then he'd be able to carry on by himself.

So it was that the slightly revised Maurice Wilson Everest Expedition made the ascent to Camp III. Here they discovered a food cache left behind by Hugh Ruttledge's expedition the previous year, and Maurice—late of the rice-water persuasion—happily gorged himself on anchovy paste, Ovaltine, sardines, King George chocolates, and other goodies from Fortnum & Mason's. One can imagine the erstwhile faster turning to his Sherpas and guiltily pressing a chocolate-smudged finger to his lips.

For the next three days a ferocious blizzard pinned them to their tents even as it threatened to blow those tents away. Then, on May 21, the blowing abruptly ceased. Rinzing and Maurice started up to Camp IV, not trotting, hardly even climbing, but mostly just clawing at the iced-up mountain. Maurice queried his companion as to the whereabouts of Ruttledge's ice steps, made the previous year. They'd found Ruttledge's chocolates, hadn't they? He seems not to have realized that a good wind can whittle ice steps into oblivion in scarcely more time than it takes to read this sentence.

Around noon they parted: Rinzing went back to Camp III while Maurice climbed on by himself. In the next few days, he distinguished himself by starting an avalanche, sliding backwards over two hundred feet of icy verglas, breaking some ribs, and accidentally destroying all his matches. When at last he staggered back to camp, he was considerably more dead than alive. But defeated? Not bloody likely! He'd just come back to pick up his Sherpas, who, he figured, might be of some use in his assault on Camp IV. But the Sherpas refused to climb even another fifty feet with him. For they'd come to the conclusion that their sahib was, at the very least, a loony.

So it ended for Maurice Wilson exactly where it began: a man alone against a mountain. No fellow climbers, no superfluous technology, not even a piton. No rice-water, either. *Alone.* The most stubborn Yorkshireman in the world against the most stubborn mountain in the world. Now we watch that man trudging wearily through the snow. Now he stands at the foot of the North Col and gazes up ...

The following year Eric Shipton, Charles Warren, and H.W. Tilman were themselves trying to reconnoiter a North Col route to the summit. It was the morning of July 9 and Warren was walking a little ahead of the others. A few hundred yards above Camp III he spotted a perfectly good pair of boots lying in the snow. Soon he saw a crumpled green tent torn from its guy ropes, along with an

LAWRENCE MILLMAN

equally crumpled Union Jack. He thought this might be an earlier expedition's dump site until he saw the body itself, huddled in the snow. "I say," he called out to Shipton, "it's that fellow Wilson ..."

Maurice was wearing—well, that's where accounts seem to differ. According to Warren, he was wearing a mauve pullover, lightweight flannel trousers, and thin socks, attire somewhat more suitable for high tea in Mayfair than the high elevations of the Himalayas. But in the next few years, another story spread: Maurice had been dressed in silken panties and a brassiere, possibly heels, too. Though the story has never been officially verified, a woman's high-heeled shoe was in fact found close to Camp III by a later expedition. Whatever Maurice's sartorial preferences, it was clear that death had come about as a result of exposure, not starvation. Which, one feels, is how this devotee of starvation would himself have preferred it.

Near the body Shipton located the weather-beaten diary in whose pages Maurice had recorded his perpetual struggle with the mountain. The entries were nearly all of a piece. "No food, no water ... terribly cold ... dead tired ... must somehow go on ..." But of how he occupied himself toward the end, or roughly when that end might have come, the diary provides not a clue. Nor does it bother to mention the deceased's taste, maybe bizarre, maybe not, in wearing apparel.

Shipton and Warren wrapped the body in its tent and slid it into a nearby crevasse, where, by all rights, it should have remained. But you can't keep a good man down. Over the years Maurice has surfaced with macabre regularity, thrust forth by the movements of Rongbuk Glacier. In 1960 Chinese climbers found him and dutifully reburied him. More recently, he's been sighted by Japanese, German, and yet more Chinese climbers. It's as if the Mother Goddess were offering her myriad visitors a bit of advice by repeatedly putting Maurice on display, as if she were telling them: Dance to the beat of your own drummer, my friends. Follow your star wherever it may lead you. And above all, keep the faith, as this gentleman himself seems to have kept it, even unto his own very cold end.

The last entry in Maurice's diary, penciled thinly but clearly, in a shaky hand, reads: "Off again, gorgeous day ..."

SNOW COUNTRY

According to local wits, Greenville, Maine, gets so much snow that it takes days, sometimes even weeks simply to shovel out what blows in through the keyhole.

There was in fact five feet of snow on the ground when I arrived in this charmingly ramshackle town, the metropolis (pop. 1,050) of Piscataquis County. Having come up from snowless Boston, I was delighted. For New England seems to me at its best, or at least its most lyrical, when it's buried under a softly luxuriant carpet of white. Never mind that when this carpet melts, it's not always easy to distinguish the roads from the rivers.

But I wanted a hands-on, or rather a feet-on, experience of snow. So I drove eight miles past Greenville to Lily Bay State Park, where I strapped on my snowshoes and tramped off into the woods. I entered a world of exquisite nothingness. There was neither movement or noise, only a frigid tranquility. If eternity is like this, I thought, I'm all for it.

In fact, nothingness is one of the chief attractions of Piscataquis County, the only county east of the Mississippi which qualifies for frontier status (five people or less per square mile) with the federal government. Since most of the county is owned by timber companies, Piscataquis tends to be mercifully free of time-sharing condos, strip malls, and car-clogged arteries of concrete. And although it's not free of clearcutting, even a clearcut landscape looks nice when it's buried under snow. Or if not actually nice, at least not so likely to inspire feelings of murderous intent toward those responsible for its rape.

A day later I strapped on my snowshoes again and started hiking along the Appalachian Trail. This ever-popular highland path passes just south of Greenville en route to its northern terminus on the summit of Katahdin, Maine's highest mountain. In the summer, I would have shared it with dozens of my fellow hikers. Now, in mid-February, I had it entirely to myself.

Well, not *entirely* to myself. The numerous tracks I saw indicated the Trail was heavily used by locals, albeit locals of the four-footed variety. Here were the bounding tracks of a rabbit, the rounded tracks of a bobcat, and a fox's doglike tracks. Here too was a porcupine's waddling track, instantly identifiable because it looks as if someone has taken a broom and brushed it back and forth in the snow. And here, probably in pursuit of the porcupine, was the track of a fisher. For a fisher, a porcupine is haute cuisine: it can ingest and pass the quills with impunity.

I doubt that I would have been aware of all this wildlife at any other time of year. For the snow was like a newspaper on which I could read the latest-breaking stories, the gossip, and the travel reports. There was even a culinary column in the form of half a deer, the other half eaten presumably by a coyote (from an animal's point of view, there are only two seasons up here, the quick and the dead).

But I was a little surprised that I hadn't come across any moose tracks. For northern Maine is quintessential moose country. Greenville itself has a Moosemania Festival complete with the crowning of a Moose Queen. There are moose in the clearcuts, moose by the lakes, and moose on the roads. And if one is to believe Indian legends, even a few of the area's mountains are moose ... or at least were moose in a prior life.

So, in the absence of an actual moose, I decided to climb a geological one—Mt. Kineo. According to the Abenaki legend, this mountain is the petrified remains of a giant moose sent down to earth by the Great Spirit to punish people for their sins. But the punishment got a bit out of hand (imagine a mountain-sized moose wreaking havoc on *your* neighborhood), so the Abenaki culture hero Glooscap vanquished it. And upon dying, it turned into this steepdown mass of rhyolite.

I persuaded a local friend, Mike Boudon, into joining me in an ascent of Kineo. We started out from the western shore of Moosehead Lake. This lake, the largest in New England, is like an inland sea. At the slightest provocation it can erupt with mountainous waves and boat-bashing winds, neither of which would be out of place in the North Atlantic. Right now, however, Moosehead's frozen, snow-covered surface offered us the peculiar, perhaps even religious pleasure of walking on water.

And pleasure it was too, despite a breeze that was like a spray of razor blades. Mike and I made our way across the lake with that typically rolling gait which makes snowshoers look like sailors just off a ship. High above us soared a bald eagle, doubtless wondering to what anomalous species these two beings with their weirdly oversized feet belonged.

Soon we came upon a group of jerrybuilt ice fishing shanties with names like "Bide-A-Wee" and "Kozy Korner." Inside each was one or more fishermen bent over a hole in the ice and waiting for the pickerel or lake trout of their dreams. Ice fishing is among the most popular rites of winter in northern New England, but it has always struck me as being a bit like a jail sentence in a cold privy.

One of the fishermen hailed us and gave us some coffee, and then to nullify its effect, cans of beer. He turned out to be another local wit. "It's so friggin' cold in here," he announced, "the water boiling on my stove just froze solid."

I grimaced. "You can do better than that," I told him.

"All right," he said. "How about this? It's so cold in here that the mercury on my thermometer went to the bottom of the glass and then two feet down that broom leaning against the wall ..."

I grimaced again. Mike grimaced, too. I think the hole in the ice grimaced as well.

Once we reached the opposite shore, we began our ascent. Up, up, up we bushwhacked, through an almost vertical maze of snow-draped evergreens. Halfway up, Mike snowshoed directly into an overhanging spruce bough. The bough's whole fragile structure of unconsolidated snow went tumbling down his back. At which he just shrugged. He'd been a medic in both Bosnia and Somalia, and getting an avalanche of snow down one's back, he said, was considerably less bothersome than being shot at.

At only 1,806 feet, Kineo is not what you would call a towering massif. But from the fire tower on its summit the entire north country stretched out dramatically before us, a panorama of pure white lakes, snow-dappled greenery, and mountains sheathed in frozen waterfalls. Off in the distance I could see the imposing bald eminence of Katahdin, a mountain so austerely beautiful that it looked more imaginary than real.

The wind was rattling the tower and thus rattling us along with it, so we headed down. Our descent went without incident until I snowshoed into a grove of alders, an experience not unlike snowshoeing into barbed wire.

Near the bottom I heard something which sounded like a cross between a giant mosquito and a chain saw. Then a flotilla of seven snowmobiles roared past us. Their helmeted drivers wore thick insulated outfits which made them look like sacks of lumpy meal ... or maybe space aliens.

I'm not a fan of snowmobiles. I can't think of anything more capable of shattering the peace of an otherwise silent, lonely place than the high-pitched whirr of their two-cycle engines. Their fumes, to my nostrils, are much worse than a skunk's. But Michael Schnetzer, my host at the Greenville Inn, was unaware of this prejudice. The first thing he said when I got back that evening was that he'd arranged a snowmobile trip for me the very next day.

So it was that I found myself installed on one of these noisy, smelly contraptions, following a guide named Paul over what seemed like most of the backcountry in Piscataquis County. We swivelled along buffed-out snowmobile trails, whisked over frozen lakes, and bounced up and down on frost heaves.

"Enjoying it?" Paul asked.

"Well, it's giving my liver a good shaking up," I said.

We ascended an icy pinnacle from which I could see the tiny insectlike forms of skiers on Big Squaw Mountain half a mile away. Then we roared across a lake with the jawbreaking Indian name of Nahmajneskicongomoc Lake. Soon we were ploughing through a clearcut that resembled a moonscape. At last we ended up at the West Shirley Bog.

Now a bog is usually not a very pleasant place to end up. You tend to get stuck in muck, trapped in slime, or swallowed up by a sinkhole. But the West Shirley Bog, at least this time of year, more or less redeemed our noisy, smelly expedition. Its snowy surface sparkled like the sun-drenched sands of a Mediterranean beach. Its dead trees had the heroic attitudes of Giacometti sculptures. And at my feet was neither muck or slime, but wind-hardened, beady snow finer than wedding rice.

The temperature was maybe ten degrees above zero, colder if you included the wind chill factor. I thought: Piscataquis County will never be the watermelon capital of North America ...

For which, I also thought, one can only be grateful.

There was still one place, neither bog, mountain, or icy pinnacle, that I wanted to visit—Chesuncook. Located forty miles northeast of Greenville, Chesuncook is the only settlement in New England, or at least mainland New England, not connected to anywhere else by a road. Granted, Chesuncook has only five year-round inhabitants (the summer population swells to around thirty), but in a country crisscrossed by highways and turnpikes, any roadless community however minuscule is remarkable.

You can reach Chesuncook only by flying in, going in by boat, or traveling there by snowmobile. Or you can drive to the end of an unmarked logging road, as I did, and snowshoe the remaining six miles. When I started this trek, the sky was overcast. An hour or so later I was trudging through a blizzard with whiteout conditions. That I didn't get deeply, perhaps irrevocably lost I can only attribute to a combination of luck and a trusty compass.

At last, after several wrong turns, I reached Chesuncook.

The falling snow gave a certain ghostly quality to a place that seemed already ghostly to begin with. There were empty houses scattered about the woods, many of them tarpapered and with rusted bed springs on their porches. A few were in such a terminally decrepit state that I felt a mere kick would have reduced them to heaps of rubble. There were a couple of others which looked slightly more habitable—these were the summer camps of people who evidently preferred rusticity to comfort.

It was hard to believe that Chesuncook had once been a thriving, turbulent lumbering outpost, one of the last of its kind. As recently as 1920, it had a population of 247. Now a bronze plaque indicated that it was on the National Register of Historic Places, proof of its obsolescence.

And yet when I dropped in on Bert and Maggie McBurney, two longtime "Suncookers," I did not feel in the presence of ghosts. They were a robust, sixty-ish couple completely at ease in their kerosene-lit log cabin. They occupied this cabin all winter, warmed only by a woodstove, and then in the spring moved to their large frame house a few hundred yards away.

Maggie, a Parisian, offered me a French tart she'd just baked. Bert, who grew up in Chesuncook, offered me stories. I heard about the local minister who claimed that rolling in the snow helped him preach. Then there was the local trapper whose house had no windows. "I don't get home until after dark and I leave before daylight," the man would tell people, "so why do I need windows?"

Bert himself couldn't imagine living anywhere else. "We have just about everything we need here," he grinned, "except civilization."

After the blizzard had run its course, I went for a walk. The air was so crisp that it virtually cleaned out my lungs. It was also very cold. *Very* cold. I felt that if I had paused to speak with a casual passerby, my words would have turned to ice in my mouth.

But there weren't any passersby in Chesuncook, casual or otherwise. The only sign of life was my own snowshoe tracks. Given the purity of the fresh snow, they almost seemed like a sacrilege. At one point I doubled back and came upon these tracks without immediately realizing they were mine. My heart skipped a beat: Was Bigfoot or an Abominable Snowman lurking somewhere nearby?

Now I headed out onto Chesuncook Lake—a giant pan of ice with a soot-black frieze of conifers on its opposite side.

All of a sudden a wolflike creature came around a wooded promontory. It was not a wolf, however. It was a coyote, an animal I'd seldom encountered in the wild before. Tracks, yes; but seldom an actual coyote. It trotted toward me, apparently preoccupied, a rare grey phantom in the pale afternoon light. A hundred feet away it stopped dead and stared directly at me for a minute, as if I were a quite rare creature myself. Then it bounded off across the lake, out of my life forever.

Snow country, I thought, is full of surprises.

A BIG CAT TALE

Nearly everyone in Riley Brook, New Brunswick, can sit you down and regale you with stories about the elusive eastern mountain lion *(Felix concolor cougar)*, known locally as panther.

Henry Leonard likes to tell about the time just last summer when, upon looking out his back window, he saw a panther advancing slowly toward his neighbor Margaret Maclean. The old woman was bent over, weeding her garden, and the animal seemed to be stalking her. Henry yelled, but she didn't hear him. Then he dashed to the phone and rang her up, which deed probably saved her. Henry now has second thoughts about doing this: A half-eaten or even a gnawed-upon Margaret would have silenced skeptics once and for all.

Elsewhere in the United States the mountain lion is, if not quite a commonplace, at least not dismissed as porch stoop legend. Perhaps four thousand manage to linger on in western canyons and remote chaparral country, with a few dozen more in the Florida Everglades. But here in the Northeast we've had a rather longer time to unfurl the so-called benefits of civilization, having cleaved, parceled, logged, manicured, and subdivided our acidy lands for 350 years. It's a wonder that we haven't eradicated even the lowly field mouse. As for panthers, the last one was trapped in 1938 by

Rosalie Morin in Somerset County, Maine. The last *official* panther, that is.

It was the unofficial panthers that prompted me to visit Riley Brook. The town was a ragamuffin scattering of rustic clapboard houses and even more rustic camps hedged in by the dense second-growth forests of the Mount Carleton highlands. A local sign read: "No dumping. Potatoes. Dead animals. Old cars." There was no development anywhere in sight: no condos, industrial parks, or country crafts. And since the demise of the Tobique Salmon Club, no money, either. In short, it seemed like just the sort of place where a much beleaguered big cat might feel comfortable hanging out.

Henry Leonard directed me to his younger brother Leroy. An eagerly voluble man, Leroy told me how he'd emerged from Sunday morning services four years ago and seen enormous round prints (the prints, definitely, of a panther, he said) circling the church in the snow, as if the animal had been debating whether or not to go in. Said Leroy: "By jingles! Wouldn't it have been something if he'd ate the minister?"

He was jesting, of course. A healthy panther would rather eat a lame deer or a stricken cow moose any day than haunch of Congregationalist minister. Indeed, a panther would probably rather eat an amphibian than a human being. A local logger named Zeke Armitage, according to Leroy, had once seen a panther climb from a roadside ditch with a frog in its mouth.

Zeke Armitage, when I visited him, said he now thought the animal in question had been a coyote, not a panther. There were plenty of coyotes in these parts, and their nocturnal caterwauling sometimes made a hash of a man's good sleep. Or it could have been a Great Dane, though God knows Great Danes were even scarcer in these parts than panthers.

Then Zeke told me another story: He'd been cutting down

timber by the Tobique River maybe thirty or forty years ago, and he'd seen this large tawny animal striding along a gravel bar "just like he owned it, Mr. Man, just like he owned it. He was an imperial animal, sure."

"Maybe it was a Great Dane," I ventured.

"You ever see a Great Dane with a ropy, two-foot tail? You ever come across one that could tolerate a temperature of 20 below? It was 20 below on that day, with the wind blowing something fierce."

"What did you do?"

"Wished him the best of luck. Not much else I could do, 'cept shoot the fella and I'd just as soon shoot my own mother, God rest her bones, as shoot a panther."

Several days later I found myself bushwhacking through the woods ten or so miles east of Riley Brook. My topo map routed me through gaunt stands of black spruce, around a hummocky sphagnum bog, over a succession of gnarly granite ledges, and down a scree slope to a lovely blue cirque called Serpentine Lake. Here I pitched my tent amid a silence so perfect that when a white-throated sparrow began singing, I wanted to thow a rock at it.

And that night, under a huge old bull moon, I tried to summon up a panther using a procedure that a Naskapi Indian elder once taught me: If you want an audience with a certain animal, either for social or culinary purposes, you must perforce turn yourself into a reasonable facsimile of that animal. Then if you've done a good job, the animal will appear to you, its consanguineous brother.

Thus I tried to turn myself into a panther. I imagined my whiskers prominent, my underparts white. I even cried out like a woman in labor, which is supposedly what a panther's cry sounds like.

Next morning I walked down to the lake to brush my teeth and there, on a ledge, lay two black elongated scats, both of which were filled with deer hair. A check of Olaus Murie's definitive handbook *Animal Tracks* presented two possibilities as to the begetter of these scats. The first was a gray wolf, which I immediately discounted, as gray wolves have been gone from New Brunswick forests since 1829. The other possibility was a panther.

I confess that I didn't bottle these scats and carry them back for positive identification by a professional scatologist. Such a person perhaps would take issue with me: he might say (for example) that the scats had been deposited by a coyote that'd bred with a gray wolf elsewhere in Canada, and now the wolf strain was coming out in the fecal matter.

By jingles! I hardly wanted to hear an explanation as eminently logical as that. Like the good citizens of Riley Brook, I wanted to believe. So I just let the scats lie there glistening in the early morning sunlight. Best to let the mystery of their origin, if mystery it be, remain intact. Best simply to make them part of a story—*this* story, in fact—in whose telling the imperial panther would once again roam the wilds, maraud, defecate, and glisten in the sunlight, as if extinction weren't forever.

AN EVENING AMONG
HEADHUNTERS

WHACK! WHACK! WHACK!

Osvaldo's machete came down with lightning rapidity on yet another hapless snake. Then he proceeded to cut it into halves, thirds, quarters, and eighths, as if he were slicing carrots for the stewpot. Thus far he'd dispatched at least two dozen snakes in this fashion. Fer-de-lances, bushmasters, even the harmless glass snake—they were all candidates for his egalitarian blade. In his enthusiasm, I think he must have done away with several liana vines and serpentine creepers, perhaps even a few epiphytes, too.

At last I got a little upset with his sanguinary behavior. I told him that he was disturbing the jungle's ecosystem by killing all these snakes. But Osvaldo, for all his virtues as a guide, was not what you would describe as an eco-minded individual. He replied:

"Have you lost a son to the bite of a bushmaster? I have lost such a son, and I am now making the snakes lose their sons. Surely you understand, Mr. Larry?"

I understood, more or less. And from then on, I kept my mouth shut about snakes. But not, definitely not, about mud. For this was the rainy season in the Ecuadorian Amazon, and the country through which we were traveling—the country of the *untsuri suarä,* or Jivaro—was not only very dense jungle, but also very dense mud. The Amazon jungle has often been described as an orgy of green. At this time of year, however, it was an orgy of brown.

For five days, our little expedition had followed a vine-choked trail that seemed more like an obstacle course than a trail. One step forward usually resulted in either being swallowed up by the mud, strangled by a vine, gored by a thorn on a vine, flayed by a gauntlet of branches, skidding backwards, skidding sideways, or even on occasion skidding down the steep embankment into the Ungamayo, a river luckily piranha-less.

On the other hand, the Ungamayo wasn't *candiru*-less. This made any type of river dip, intentional or otherwise, a hazard. For the candiru is a fish that makes the better-known piranha seem as innocuous as a Barbie doll. Also known as "the toothpick fish," it swims up the urethra and then extends its spiny retrorse fins, where-upon it becomes agonizingly undislodgable. If you don't get to a hospital right away, your bladder will burst. And if you don't hap-pen to be anywhere near a hospital, your only recourse is to find someone capable of administering last rites.

The balsa log bridges we came upon seemed to have been de-signed for river dips of the unintentional variety. We were con-vinced that they'd been coated with grease just prior to our arrival. In trying to cross them, we must have looked like a parade of spas-tic tightrope walkers. On one of these crossings, our ethnobotanist Paul Cunnane slipped off the log and landed with a splat in a pool of blackish ooze, only to reappear a few moments later looking as if he'd just lost a skirmish with a mud slide in his native California.

"Goddamfuckinsonafabitch!" Cunnane yelled. (Or something equally passionate. I wasn't taking notes at the time.)

"Ah, another expletive for our peerless guide," declared Petrie. Osvaldo, part Jivaro and part Ecuadorian, was very eager to learn English language swear words on the assumption that they would come in quite handy if he ever went to America. Every time one of us swore, he would politely ask for the words to be repeated. Then he would repeat the word or phrase himself, the better to remember it.

Ever onward into the jungle we slipped, skidded, slopped, and fell, swearing and then swearing again for Osvaldo's benefit, a quartet of white men en route to a rendezvous with the fabled Jivaro. At this rendezvous, Cunnane planned to drink *natemä (Banisteriopsis caapi)*, the hallucinogenic drug that puts the Jivaro in touch with their ancestors. He hoped to get in touch with a few of their ancestors himself, and then write up the encounter for his ethnobotanical journal.

None of the rest of us was into drugs, at least not with the same degree of scholarly rigor. Petrie, an anthropologist, preferred lascivious subjects like puberty rites and genital scarification. Lethbridge was a British Columbia museum curator who wanted to purchase a few chonta palm *cerbatanas* (blowguns) and curare darts, perhaps a shrunken monkey or sloth's head as well, for his special collections.

As for myself, I'd joined the expedition for what is commonly referred to as "the experience." Jack Petrie, who'd invited me to come along, had been a friend of mine since college; he told me that the trip would be, as he put it, "a perfectly splendid ordeal." My previous trip had been a trek into the Labrador outback; a trek where I'd gotten lost, been eaten alive by sky-darkening clouds of black flies and mosquitoes, and strained at least two ligaments. This jungle adventure, Petrie promised me, would equal and possibly surpass that one for sheer physical discomfort.

And discomfort there certainly was, especially when we stopped. It was then that endless relays of konga ants would come up and pay their respects to us.

"Osvaldo may not like snakes," Lethbridge observed, "but he

LAWRENCE MILLMAN

doesn't seem to mind konga ants at all. You'll notice how he always picks their campsites for our campsite ..."

Lethbridge did not have a very high opinion of konga ants. The words "genocide" and "holocaust" kept escaping from his lips whenever he mentioned them. But then none of us had a high opinion of konga ants. They'd get onto our bodies and clamp their pincers into some exposed bit of skin, then inject venom from a stinger in the rear of their abdomens. This venom, whose presence made itself felt for hours on end, served to raise the decibel level of our expletives several notches.

Petrie would try to keep up our spirits by saying that the bite of a konga ant was actually quite pleasant compared to the way we'd feel with a candiru lodged in the urethra.

But Cunnane wasn't having any of this optimism. Every time an ant bit him, he would subject the f-word to various permutations and combinations that I would not have thought humanly possible.

Osvaldo was thus highly versed in our vernacular by the time we reached a little clearing in the jungle. Here stood the fifty-foot-long *chacra* that was our destination. It was built of stout chonta palm staves set vertically in the ground an inch or so apart, with closely woven palm thatch for a roof. This roof rose to perhaps twenty feet in the center. There were no windows, as the Jivaro think windows a needless extravagance, not to mention an invitation for four-legged and two-legged enemies to climb in.

We paused outside and Osvaldo shouted in falsetto: "*Whee-dee! Whee-dee!* There are five of us, and we are friendly." Then he waited, silently regarding but not removing a tapir tick that was crawling up his arm.

From inside the chacra came the reply: "*Whee-dee!* You are welcome."

And what if we had not been friendly? Well, it's been a quarter of a century since the Jivaro shrank down the heads of unwelcome guests to the size of softballs. At least it's been that long since they did it as an integral part of their culture rather than simply to stay in practice. But even then they didn't bother to shrink the heads of white men. For white men, they believed, did not possess souls. And if the whole point of headshrinking was to render your enemy's soul small and thus manageable upon its reincarnation, shrinking a white man's head was unnecessary, indeed wholly redundant.

So it was that we entered the chacra with a reasonable certainty that we would leave it with our heads still joined to our necks and likewise the same size as before.

Once inside, we hunkered down on log benches behind which stood a row of six-foot-long arrows with sharp curare-blackened tips. Osvaldo introduced us to the man of the house, Juanga. Juanga was dressed in green Adidas running shorts, a dirty polyester T-shirt that advertised the Galapagos, and Wellington boots. This wardrobe, Osvaldo informed us, was a present from the Belgian missionaries who occasionally dropped in on the Jivaro. Juanga's personal accessories also included a jaguar fang necklace. This, I assumed, was not a present from the missionaries.

We bowed our heads slightly toward him (shaking hands, Osvaldo had warned us, is a summons to battle), and he bowed toward each of us in his turn. Half a dozen naked kids with bellies swollen over their malarial spleens, the resident shaman, Juanga's younger brother Cajeke, leatherfaced old men, women with drooping triangular breasts, even some abject and scrawny dogs—all of them studied us intently. With our bush costumery and various ethno-appurtenances, we were real weird, man.

Now Juanga's wife came over to us. She was dressed in a red loincloth and wore a pudding-basin haircut. She dipped a gourd into a bucket of *nijamanchi* (Spanish: *chicha*) and then offered it ceremoniously to her husband, who drank it and gave the gourd back to her, thus demonstrating for us guests that it wasn't poisoned. She filled the gourd again and this time offered it to Osvaldo, who drank it even as he took care to avert his eyes from her face. It is considered very rude for a guest to acknowledge a Jivaro woman.

Nijamanchi is home brew. *Home* brew. It's made from fermented yucca (manioc) root that's been chewed to a pulp by the woman of the house. The woman's oral bacteria contributes to the fermentation process, something which Lethbridge, for one, did not appreciate. When his turn came, he refused the gourd. In doing so, he used Latin names to invoke the wide range of germs, some lethal, others merely dangerous, that the brew doubtless harbored. But Osvaldo got back the gourd for him.

Lethbridge shook his head. "The number of parasite eggs in that gourd positively boggles the mind," he said.

"It is very bad manners not to drink," Osvaldo told him.

"And bad manners are a crime the Jivaro punish by death," added Petrie cheerfully. "In fact, you may even reawaken their headhunting urge."

Muttering to himself, Lethbridge drank.

Now it was my turn. The woman offered me the gourd, and I took a few tentative sips. Not bad, I thought. Not bad at all. It tasted like a marriage between buttermilk and beer, with a subtle aftertaste of spit. I slowly drank the contents of the gourd, and then the woman returned to the bucket and filled it up again. I tried to indicate that I didn't want any more, but that isn't easy when you're scrupulously looking every which way but at the person whose attention you're trying to get.

One thing about nijamanchi: it gives your bladder a full workout. Cunnane was the last to get the gourd. I waited until after he'd drunk and then I rose to go outside. And as I left the chacra, Juanga's youngest son got up and joined me. He was observing the Jivaro custom which requires that a member of the family accompany a guest to the lavatory (any area not under cultivation), and chat amiably with him while he answers Nature's call. The boy and I could not chat amiably since we didn't share a common language, but at least we were keeping up appearances.

When we returned to the chacra, the boy uttered some words in Shuar, the Jivaro language, to Osvaldo. Osvaldo turned to me and said:

"What's wrong with your penis?"

"Inertia, mostly," I replied.

"No, the boy says part of it is missing. He wonders if a *brujo* tried to get a candiru out and made a mistake."

As best I could, I explained the role of circumcision in my culture, citing studies that show circumcised males have lower rates of urinary tract infections and sexually transmitted diseases than males who have not undergone the knife. A look of incredulity crept across Osvaldo's face. Lopping off a man's head was one thing, but lopping off a portion of his virile member was quite another. I had no choice but to step back outside and expose myself. Osvaldo's incredulity did not go away.

"The foreskin is a relatively insensitive piece of skin," I told him.

"How would you know, Mr. Larry?" he said. "You don't have one."

In our absence the story of my missing foreskin had gone the rounds of the chacra. And upon our return there was a riff of giggling and glottal-stopping banter at my expense. A woman with a baby sucking at her breast was so convulsed with laughter that she almost fell out of her split-vine sleeping-net. Even a couple of naked toddlers were laughing and pointing at me. Evidently, it was not considered bad manners to ridicule guests if they happened to be, like me, freaks of nature.

"This guy's a laughingstock in his own country, too," said Petrie. Osvaldo translated for the others.

"You're going to get a very nasty letter from my lawyer when we get back," I told Petrie.

Meanwhile the shaman had gone outside with Cunnane and now he came back to report that Cunnane's member, unlike mine, was intact.

"Some of us happen to be circumcised, some of us not, and Mr. Cunnane wasn't, probably because his background is Irish," I explained. Osvaldo dutifully translated this statement, but I could have been talking about floppy disks or cast-iron flamingo lawn ornaments just as readily as ethnic differences. Among whites, the Jivaro make no distinctions. Except for me. I'd become an instant anthropological specimen.

The shaman said something to Osvaldo and gestured in my direction.

"The brujo wants to know whether you are maybe a type of homosexual person," Osvaldo asked me.

"I'm not any type of homosexual person. Why does the brujo think that?"

"Because there is an old legend among our people. Many years ago one of our gods was a homosexual person. He had a very long penis, maybe a hundred feet long, and he kept sticking it into other men. That way he could capture their souls and put them into a little box. The sun god Etsa decided that it was very wrong for him to do this, so he snapped some of his penis off. And the part he snapped off became the grandfather of all the poisonous snakes in the world."

"Please tell the brujo that my penis has not been snapped off by any sun god," I said.

Osvaldo related what I'd said to the shaman, who immediately replied in Shuar. Then Osvaldo said, "The brujo will be glad to restore your missing part ... for a price."

"What price?"

The two of them conferred. Then Osvaldo said, "One stereo cassette tape recorder. Or maybe a bolt-action rifle."

Politely but firmly I declined the offer, though I must say that I was curious about what hocus-pocus, sleight-of-hand, or medicinal herbs the shaman would have used to restore my long-lost prepuce.

"The brujo says that if you die in this incomplete state," Osvaldo went on, "you will be reborn without a leg or an arm. And then when you are reborn after that, it might be without *both* legs ..."

Now dinner was announced. This brought at least a temporary halt to the mockery of my anatomy. On the chacra's dirt floor Juanga's wife had set a couple of huge banana fronds, and we helped ourselves to a spread of piranha, yams, yucca, and taro root, all boiled in the same pot and tasting pretty much the same. The palm grub side dish I could have done without. But the entree, howler monkey roasted whole, had a gamey flavor which I found rather tasty. According to Petrie, this flavor was not unlike the flavor of roasted *Homo sapiens.*

He should know. Once, on a field trip to Irian Jaya, he'd unwittingly dined on chunks of a dead warrior whom one of his ethnosubjects had killed. The similarity of those chunks to monkey, which he'd eaten earlier in the trip, had proved to him once and for all the accuracy of Darwin's theories about human origins. Indeed, he often used this similarity as an opener when he lectured college students on evolution.

While we ate, Cunnane fasted. An hour after dinner, the shaman was ready with the natemä. Cunnane was instructed to remove his clothing.

"Have a good trip, pal," Petrie told him.

First Cunnane inhaled some greenish nasal snuff (*tsangu*), which made him grimace. Then he took a nip of natemä, which made him throw up. But this the Jivaro would argue was not so much throwing up as it is getting rid of one's evil spirits.

Cunnane took more nips and got rid of more evil spirits. His last batch of evil spirits were personally disposed of by the shaman, who put his mouth to Cunnane's navel, sucked loudly and then spat. This brought shouts of merriment from the kids in the chacra.

"Why are they laughing?" I whispered to Osvaldo. "Is it because they think it's silly to perform this sort of ancient ritual nowadays?"

"Oh no," he said. "They do not think it's silly at all. They are laughing because they've never seen their brujo get rid of a white man's evil spirits before. Maybe they think it's a really big job ..."

Thus purged of evil spirits, Cunnane drank a little more of the natemä, which he now seemed able to keep down. Then the shaman shook a dried barbasco sprig over various parts of his body and began chanting something in a voice that became increasingly eerie and distant, although once or twice it erupted into the roar of, I assumed, a jaguar. I noticed that his eyes were glazed, as if he'd previously been taking some of the natemä himself.

"By now you should be floating above your body," Osvaldo told Cunnane.

"I'm not floating anywhere," Cunnane replied, green tsangu slime trickling out of his nostrils.

"Then perhaps you are seeing some wild animals? A big jaguar, for example?"

"Nope, nothing."

Natemä has powerful hallucinogenic alkaloids which produce a narcotized state similar to the mescaline of the peyote cactus. A good trip often includes visions of fighting jaguars or other heroic beasts, followed by an audience with one's ancestors; a bad trip, visions of gigantic spiders with hairy twisted faces or perhaps snakes with human faces, followed by an audience with one's enemies. But as the evening wore on, it was apparent that Cunnane's trip consisted of nothing more dramatic than an upset stomach, of which he kept complaining. The natemä, he said, had the same effect on him as a greasy pizza. Petrie took his pulse. It was normal.

"You are *really* not seeing any jaguars?" Osvaldo said, a look of amazement on his face.

"None at all," Cunnane said.

Now Osvaldo and the shaman got into a discussion in Shuar. I assumed Osvaldo was telling him that he'd given his charge, instead of the usual ancestral fix, indigestion. Soon the discussion turned into an argument, which turned into a shouting match, at least on Osvaldo's side. The shaman himself only shrugged and shook his head decisively. So decisively that it sent a ripple effect through his whole body right down to his calloused feet, which he stamped angrily.

At one point I thought Osvaldo was going to hit him. Fortunately, he didn't. To hit a Jivaro shaman would be rather like decking the Pope. Very bad juju.

Osvaldo told us the problem. Cunnane had received only about one-third the recommended dose of natemä, which was not enough to get a konga ant high, much less a full-blooded ethnobotanist. The shaman was refusing to give him more because he had no idea what a white man could tolerate. White men, he said, were different from the Jivaro, and an overdose might scramble Cunnane's brains for good, possibly even kill him. And then the Ecuadorian government would not be happy.

"Who cares if the Ecuadorian government is happy?" said Petrie. "I mean, we're about as far removed from any political arena here as you can possibly get."

"The brujo cares," replied Osvaldo. "He went to jail some years ago because he took another man's head, and he does not want to go to jail again."

"Tell the brujo that I'll take full responsibility for anything that happens," Cunnane said.

But it was too late. The shaman had already gathered his effects into a vine-bound medicine-bag and recanted the rest of the natemä. I caught one last glimpse of his primal Asiatic face before he left. A face whose lines were folded and then folded again into a ruinous splendor. The face of a man much saddened by these headless modern times.

One by one, my companions turned in. Just before I joined them, I went outside to empty my bladder again. It was a very clear night, with the Southern Cross pinned three-dimensionally to the sky and the stars around it so bright that they seemed to hum with wattage. Monkeys screeched; frogs croaked; insects sang; and a small bird made a series of soft whisking trajectories above me.

This time my lavatorial companion was Juanga's brother Cajeke, a fiercely-painted man who looked as if his hobby was disemboweling grandmothers with his machete. And as I stood there relieving myself, suddenly Cajeke raised his machete.

Holy shit! I thought. He's going to reenact the myth of the sun god on my poor abused organ of generation. But then he brought the machete down with a WHACK! on a five-foot fer-de-lance which was slithering directly toward me from across the yucca plantation. Cajeke's blow neatly severed the snake, whereupon both parts writhed convulsively for a few moments and then grew still.

From now on, I decided, I'd always be grateful for the etiquette of headhunters.

ABOUT THE
AUTHOR

✤

LAWRENCE MILLMAN has written for *Smithsonian, National Geographic, Sports Illustrated,* and numerous other magazines. His books include *Our Like Will Not Be There Again, Hero Jesse, A Kayak Full of Ghosts,* and *Last Places.* When not on the road, he lives in Cambridge, Massachusetts.